GOOD
for Goodness' Sake

*7 Values for Cultivating
Authentic Character
in Midlife*

GOOD
for Goodness' Sake

Gary Fenton

new
hope
PUBLISHERS

New Hope® Publishers
P. O. Box 12065
Birmingham, AL 35202-2065
www.newhopepublishers.com

Library of Congress Cataloging-in-Publication Data

Fenton, Gary.
 Good for goodness' sake : 7 values for cultivating authentic character
in midlife / Gary Fenton.
   p. cm.
 ISBN 1-59669-009-7 (jacketed hardcover)
  1. Character. 2. Values. 3. Virtues. 4. Good and evil. 5.
 Middle-aged persons—Conduct of life. I. Title.
 BJ1518.F46 2006
 170.84'4—dc22
               2006011863

ISBN: 1-59669-009-7

N064135 • 0806 • 5M1

Dedication

This book is dedicated to Dr. George Brown whose passion for excellence is matched only by his compassion for his patients and their families. Instead of allowing himself to be defined by what he had accomplished in his past, he chose to be known for his vision for the future. Dr. Brown taught me to dream bigger, to risk more, and that having faith in God means to trust God's people. His statement "You know you are old when you choose to act out of convenience rather than conviction" has encouraged me to stay young by seeking good for goodness' sake.

Table of Contents

CHAPTER 1

In Search of Goodness

OVER FOUR HUNDRED "MOVERS, SHAKERS, and wannabes" attended the January meeting of a leadership organization. The organization was noted for the outstanding guest speakers who addressed significant leadership, business, and government issues. The colorful printed program promised that this month's meeting was consistent with the organization's excellent reputation.

The guest speaker's picture was on the front of the program. The biographical information on the inside indicated that he was a corporate whiz from a fast-growing company whose success was the envy of all. The chair at the head table on the platform, normally reserved for the guest personality, was empty. The master of ceremonies was obviously doing a verbal tap dance, stalling for time while continuing to furtively glance toward the room's main entrance. He may not have been thinking religious thoughts, but he was certainly looking for a savior to arrive. There was obviously no Plan B if the speaker was a no-show.

A waiter wearing a black coat, starched shirt, and

bow tie handed the master of ceremonies a note. The relief on his face was like an Arizona sunrise. The master of ceremonies announced with a smile, "We have just been informed today's speaker has had a slight delay, but he is in the building and will be ready to speak in less than five minutes. While we wait for his arrival, will each of you tell the other persons at your table what your number one goal is for the New Year?"

This was not a gathering of "touchy feely/share your pain" folks, but of men and women who believed in the old-school leadership style of "I will tell you what I want you to know when I want you to know it." There was an awkward silence at my table. Finally, a man who was about 50 years old said, "My number one goal for the year is to become a better person. What advice would you give me?" Everyone at our table just sat there trying to think of some witty self-help line. But the man, his voice cracking with emotion, interrupted our silence with, "I am serious about this. I don't think I am really a bad person, but how do I start to become a really good person?" The guest speaker appeared and rescued us from the man in search of goodness.

The speaker had about 10 minutes worth of material but spoke for 25 minutes. His bumper crop of words was surrounded by a famine of humility. The audience was as relieved when the speaker finished as the master of ceremonies had been when he arrived. At the conclusion of the program, the man with the question at my table said to me, almost apologetically, "That speaker illustrated what I mean. I don't think he was a bad person, but neither do I think he was that good. I think I, as well as almost anyone in this room, could have delivered the same speech. I know how to make money, organize my time, live longer, feel better, do good things, and even be religious. But I want to do more than do good things. I want to be a good person. I guess it may sound childish and immature, but I want to be a good person, genuinely good. To be honest, goodness has not been very important to me until this stage of life, and I don't think I am that different than most of my peers."

Can You Be a Good Person?

This man may have asked the real question of midlife, "How can I be a good person?" He is not the only person asking the question. Although those who are pondering this issue come from many different social, economic, and racial backgrounds, I have found that the ones who are talking to me about this question are baby boomers, those folks born after 1945 and prior to 1968. It may be because I fit in this age group, or it could be the result of that group being such a large generation, but for whatever the reason, the greatest number of people I find facing that question are those who immediately followed the G.I. Joe and the Greatest Generation. While they do not always say the words, "How can I be good?" they are definitely facing issues of character.

Through my work as a pastor and by being involved in the community, I found that many conversations have a common thread. As I read the letters we received through our television ministry and after I spoke at several leadership conferences, I noticed the same issues were appearing over and over. In conversations with several health care professionals, human resources managers, and professional counselors, it appeared we were experiencing a real crisis in character development.

> *I sense we have a large group of people who really want to be good for goodness' sake but are unsure of how to get there.*

There was a whole generation of folks who appeared lost in life but still had the energy and interest to find their way. I am by no means an expert on the subject of character development, and I certainly recognize my own character limitations. My training and experience have equipped me to be a pastor who hears the burdens, ambitions, and hurts of saints and sinners. In the course of my journey, however, I sense we have a large group of people who really want to be good for goodness' sake but are unsure of how to get there.

I hear this yearning in many stories. A physician, who jokingly said the only reason he volunteered to go on a mission trip to Africa was because they promised he could treat people and not have to deal with government and insurance paper work, told me on his return that he felt the purpose of going was to find his soul. A 45-year-old attorney who is proud of her career achievements said surely there is something more meaningful in life beyond saying, "I have made it and look at me." The social worker who told me, "On my worst days I realize almost every good act I have done was for selfish purposes. Before I go, I want to know I have done something good for the right reason without expectation of reward." Even the mother who said, "My exterior life has been consistently good, meaning that I have not created problems for husband, children, or friends, but I really do not like who I am on the inside. Looking back, I have done good things out of fear and not out of faith."

All of these folks are using different words to ask the same question, "How can I become a good person?" It is more than latent desire for perfection. I do not find many in midlife who have any illusions of perfection. The illusion of perfection left in the stage of life when bad complexion arrived.

The Tasks of Midlife

While finding and claiming identity is the task of the first quarter of life, acceptance by others is the assignment of the second quarter, and bestowing blessing is the duty of the final quarter, the third quarter is marked by the building of character for character's sake. To some extent, character is birthed earlier in life and is continually expanding in every stage of life. But character takes a new shape after we have claimed who we are and can articulate who we are to others. Often we realize the character we formed in the earlier stages of life was not value-based but a reflection of ourselves driven by our passion for acceptance, success, and survival.

The pressures applied by external sources such as parents, teachers, and peers often form our character in the first twenty years of life. With a combination of idealism and need for approval of peers and authority figures, we assumed that if we were good or at least gave the appearance of being good, people would like us. After college and into our late 30s, our character is often very utilitarian. We want our children, supervisors, and clients to know that our character is good because we know the right kind of character will produce good kids, a boost up the mobility ladder, and a wholesome reputation that opens the door of opportunity for our career and in the community. We are good because it is effective public relations and it works.

But sometime in the third 20-year period of life, the external pressure to develop good character is minimized. We can hide our bad character. We read the books we want, watch movies and television in the privacy or secrecy of our homes, and cruise the Internet without the fear that we are polluting the minds of our children. We are adults and we are no longer required to protect our innocent minds from that which may later harm us. "Later" is here now. We have more discretionary income with fewer mouths to feed, feet to shoe, and teeth to brace, so we can be wasteful without feeling guilty. It is our money and we are not taking food off of our kids' table or limiting their education when we spend it.

Our stewardship character in the past may have been fueled by necessity rather than a chosen value. Frequently we are at a level in our organization or company where we are no longer expected to be "lean and hungry." Our work ethic becomes more practical than principled. We can coast using the momentum of yesterday to push us toward tomorrow's finish line. People have already formed their opinion of us; good character really will not produce measurable change in our income or prestige. Our mothers always wanted us to be normal, and we are! We are just like many other midlifers who have worked the past 40 years growing up and who are

> *Is it any wonder, then, that many people implode during this midlife window that is often called "the adolescence of adulthood"?*

now asking, "Is this why I neglected my family, stepped on my colleagues, short-changed friendships, and rented my soul?"

Is it any wonder, then, that many people implode during this midlife window that is often called "the adolescence of adulthood"? Adolescence is the stage of life in which experimentation is common and we realize that neither are we small children, nor are we adults. Baby boomers are finding that midlife again is a new time of experimentation. A motivational speaker who frequently speaks to baby boomers describes adolescence as "when your body is capable of getting married and having babies, but your mind and your soul are too young for either marriage or sex. Growing up is when you choose to allow your mind and soul to direct the actions of the body." This "shoot from the hip" speaker might describe midlife maturity as the time when you choose to let your character determine your conduct rather than allowing your circumstances to determine your character.

The Second Adolescence

Midlifers, like youths in adolescence, appear to be joining the addiction lines in record numbers. Just as teenagers, as they gradually remove the restraints of childhood, are willing to experiment with actions that potentially can become addictive, so are adults, whose actions are no longer observed by their children. Alcohol, prescription drugs, pornography, and a variety of sexual addictions are no longer only the property of the young, the poor, and the wounded warriors.

Once the baby boomers reached their late 20s, the rate of violent crimes decreased; but when these postwar kids began hitting their 40s and 50s, white-collar crimes increased. The bad boys of Wall Street and corporations like Enron, WorldCom, and HealthSouth had many folks indicted who had children in college or small grandchildren. These folks no longer refilled their birth control pill prescriptions at the neighbor pharmacy, but discreetly ordered up their vitamins, Viagra, and other vitality fixes at out-of-town pharmacies or on the Internet. The accused felons in these Wall Street scams were generally too old to claim ignorance and too young to plead dementia, because most of those indicted were between 38 and 60 years of age. The financial community could produce a video, "Baby

Boomers Gone Wild on Wall Street," that would rank right up there in moral decadence any other "Gone Wild" videos sold on cable television. Instead of the cameras focusing on college students without clothes, their lenses would be directed toward baby boomers without character.

The players in the drama of midlife decadence are not limited to the business world. The religious clerics accused of abusing children, the college coaches accused of cheating in recruiting, and the people in media accused of creating news rather than reporting it are often in a similar age category. During their youth, the early baby boomers were frequently accused of being a generation of teenaged delinquents. Of course, not all people in this age bracket are deeply flawed in character, but far too many people think that if we just stop perverts from downloading from the Internet, help politicians define "is," and keep the clergy away from kids, we can control the character crisis in our nation.

For the Right Reasons

The man in the opening story asked the real question of midlife: "How can I be a good person?" The primary quest at every stage of life should be goodness, and that goodness is more than legalistically performing good deeds. At the early stages of life there are so many forces pushing us to do good and right things, and for that we are grateful. But is there a goodness that flows out of our hearts not motivated by fear or a desire to meet someone else's expectations? Without a protective parent pushing us, a charismatic youth minister inspiring us, or an older supervisor looking over our shoulder, at midlife we have the opportunity to become a person of character with no reward other than knowing you are a person of character.

> *At midlife we have the opportunity to become a person of character with no reward other than knowing you are a person of character.*

Wasn't that what we once thought adulthood really was? Back when we believed that adults were people who did right because they wanted to and not because their parents, coaches, and principals made them? While some may think midlife is about coasting, it can be a very productive time of life and possibly the most fertile time growing the soul and the seat of goodness. Midlife can be the best time to address our character and to develop the virtue of goodness. For some it may be the first time they have chosen to develop their own character rather than mimic the character of those around them.

How do you become a good person when there is no external force requiring you to do so? How do you become good for goodness' sake?

Good for goodness' sake is not found by accident. It begins by intentionally choosing the values that will govern your actions. The 2004 election has caused both political parties in America to strategically work values language into carefully crafted sound bites.

Folks on the left and right wings of the political landscape are encouraging us to live by our values, and even the education industry is now beginning to acknowledge that values do have a place in the education process. Quality character is thought to be the end result of consistently living by your values. Although the process is now given many names, most discussions on values and character are reformulation and restatements of the values clarification movement that was prominent in the past. "Define your values and then try to live by them" is sometimes called the eleventh commandment.

But there is a dirty little secret about determining your values and trying to live by them. The truth is that people for the most part do live or act out their values—not the truths they tell pollsters in election years, or the values they affirm in their places of worship, but the truths around which they plan their day. You really do not need to tell people to live by their values, because they do. Bad people choose actions consistent with their values, and the reason their actions are bad is because their values are bad. Good people do good deeds because they are acting out their good values. Before values are defined, we need to carefully choose them. Often we have inherited a value system from families, peers, or society, and defining them simply means we choose which ones we will live by and which ones we will ignore.

But what happens when our values are flawed to begin with? And what about folks like us who are good sometimes and bad sometimes? This happens because down deep our trump card value is usually not good.

The most commonly held value is assuming that whatever works is valuable. This explains how we can do both good and bad in the name of values. Using an old line from the television show *M.A.S.H.*, spineless Frank Burns says, "It is nice to be nice to the nice." Burns's statement is from American Pragmatism 101, which taught us to be good to people and they will be good to us.

We can explain why we do things to our family and friends and even occasionally our enemies. But the cliché "You have to do what you have to do" explains why and how we justify manipulation, dishonesty, breaking legal contracts, and betraying binding vows to the people who are not nice. The negative phrasing of Frank Burns' statement could be "You have to fight fire with fire."

When good people surround us, we survive and thrive by doing good. But if doing good doesn't help us get ahead, we perceive that we are justified in getting even. If kindness gets in the way of our more immediate agenda of meeting our felt needs, we can easily default to greed, consumption, and exploitation. We then become just like the people we criticize when we are gossiping with our good friends about the people who are bad.

Instruction to live by our values, although well-meaning, often does not bring about long-term behavior change. This occurs because the flaw is not in our external behavior mechanism, but in our very core values. Our actions are the logical result of what we believe to be most valuable. When our character is exposed, the weakness is not the delivery system, but the infrastructure of our soul. To be a good person requires us to have good values.

The Core of Our Values

Often what we understood to be core values in our youth and early adulthood were in reality little more than rules for specific circumstances. We were taught to obey our parents, to act respectfully toward our elders and authorities, to be honest, and perhaps even to be religious. Although those rules are good, they often are more related to a core value of upward mobility. We knew that if we followed these rules, we were on our way to having as much success and recognition as anyone else. If we were really good at these rules, we might surpass everyone and arrive at the altar of success before the slower people, or as we sometimes called them, "people with bad character." These rules are seen as both the exit door from the land of the average and the entrance door to the holy land of privilege and respectability.

It is at this point that many middle-aged baby boomers realize that something has eluded them. They are successful because they have better homes than their parents, own two SUVs, participate in a vested retirement plan, and with a few notable exceptions, are respected by their colleagues at work and the strangers they call neighbors. As they look at their "fan club," these midlifers realize they do not really respect the people who respect them. As one 50-year-old attorney said to me, "I realize that I have worked most of my professional life trying to be respected by people I don't respect." The old Groucho Marx line "I refuse to join any club that would have me as a member" is not only humorous but true to many who are in search of goodness.

Before you attribute this attitude entirely to cynicism, look to see if it has some roots in your perspective gained through midlife. By the time we have lived through at least 40 Decembers, we realize that some of the folks who play the role of Santa Claus are really old codgers who would rather sit in soft chairs at department stores than get a real job. They may not be people who like kids as much as people who dislike real work. We also realize that those we have expected to play "Santa Claus" or "Sugar Daddy" for us may have been using us more than we were using them. The supervisors who were going to promote us out the of the dull and drudgery department up to the division designed for the exciting and entrepreneurial may have expected youthful enthusiasm to be their meal ticket out of their own mid-management world. The community activist who praised us because of our love for the downtrodden may have been stepping on our backs to help him build his not-for-profit organization, or a least to get a larger share of next year's United Way budget. We have learned to see the dark side of the superstars in the office and the community. We realize that all that glitters may not be gold; often, it is just glitter.

In early 2005, a sportswriter who had for several years defended the boorish and crude remarks of a well-known college basketball coach whose behavior embarrassed his school now encouraged the school to fire the coach. In the writer's Internet column, he urged the university president to fire the coach and encouraged the coach to look at the kind of man he had become and asked if maybe that was the kind of man he had been all along.

Experience makes us realize that the "rosy cheeks" of innocence on others may be more the result of our own rose colored glasses than of virtue on display.

This formerly cheerleading journalist at midlife is now realizing that not every winning coach is a winner. Had the journalist been a naïve Homer who was blinded by the national championship trophies and coach-of-the-year honors? Perhaps, but a more realistic assessment is that the writer hit midlife and now had the experience to know a jerk when he met one. Experience makes us realize that the "rosy cheeks" of innocence on others may be more the result of our own rose colored glasses than of virtue on display.

Yet unbridled cynicism is not a mark of goodness. The self-righteous cynic hits middle age and doubts the virtue of everyone else. These folks become suspicious "know it alls," as so powerfully portrayed by the character "Archie Bunker" in the *All in the Family* television series. It is interesting to note that Archie Bunker was the ultimate antihero to high school and college students 25 to 35 years ago. Now these same students are facing the same life issues Archie was when they loved to hate him. He dealt with being the parent of a college student, the marriage of a daughter, age-related changes in his work assignment, and the birth of a grandchild. These are the same life issues that the baby boomers are confronting today. Archie was not in search of goodness, for in his own mind he had achieved goodness. This was why the youth so despised him. At midlife you have to ask, "Have I become Archie Bunker? Is the reason I am not seeking good character because I think I already have it?"

An authentic search for good character will require you to recognize that you also have the potential to be and become what you once despised. The true searcher for goodness who looks through the lens of healthy cynicism will look at the mirror as well as out the window.

The journey toward goodness is not easy. It requires continual self-examination. Yet today, religious folks are more noted for examining the lives of others and the direction of the culture instead of prescribing cures for character sickness they see in themselves.

Specks and Planks

Jesus frequently called His disciples to examine their motives. In one of the more powerful word pictures in the Gospel of Matthew, Jesus warned the disciples against focusing their attention on the speck in their brother's eye while ignoring the plank in the their own eyes. These words are spoken to the disciples who, until they followed Jesus, saw their religious leaders model good rules but not be good people. The most consistent enemies of Jesus were scribes and Pharisees who followed the rules of goodness and legalistically made the rituals daily standard operating procedure. They were the "Archie Bunkers" of the time. Observing their painfully good behavior was probably a great source of entertainment to the residents of the first century. This may explain why American television ridicules Christians, because it reflects what Americans see everyday in the workplace and in their communities.

At midlife, we not only have enough experience for healthy cynicism, but we also have a realistic expectation of living long enough to make changes. Just 100 years ago, a 45-year-old knew he was fortunate if he had 20 years left. Today, the 45-year-old knows that if he does not already have a serious health problem, he should expect to live between 35 and 40 more years. Depending upon which gerontology expert you read, women who reach 50 without life-threatening illness are expected to make it to any age between 85 and 92. Men who are in good health at 50 should expect to remain active until their early to mid 80s.

Middle age was once the gateway to goodbye; now it is statistically accurate to say it really is the middle of life. As a gentleman who just turned 50 told me, he realized that he did not like who he was and also realized that if he didn't change, he was going to have to live with a man he didn't like for 40 more years. If you think you are facing death, you will likely be more interested in being forgiven than in being of good character. But if you are facing 40 more years of life, you have the time to search and find the virtue of goodness in and of itself.

Life without good character is a burden. A well-known journalist and author who prided himself in riding roughshod over those he interviewed committed suicide. His suicide was not an irrational act and not caused by the loss of health or by rejection. It was a carefully planned action. He had repeatedly told his family that he would end his life when he saw the first evidence that his career skills were diminishing, and he kept his word. A local writer who knew the deceased journalist said in a local media outlet regarding his friend's suicide, "I think he just grew weary of being obnoxious."

Society will tolerate and include a youth with bad character because they assume experience will be a firm but gentle teacher. But society will isolate the mature adult with bad character, and if at midlife you have 40 years left, that is a long time to be isolated or lonely. The bad news is that many of our generation have neglected character development, but the good news is that there is still time.

> *Life without good character is a burden.*

If you do live by your values, regardless of what they are, what values do you need in order to live the good life and how do you acquire or develop these virtues? In the next few chapters we start the journey toward goodness for goodness' sake. We will look at virtues that will help us be good. By no means are the virtues discussed in this book the only ones we need to cultivate in midlife. They are simply virtues in which many of our generation appear to be deficient.

Each of these values will lead us to other values as well. Character is not developed by following a list of rules. The issues are interconnected, however, and when we grow in one, it should lead us to grow in others as well. These virtues will not necessarily make you wealthy or happy, but they can help you be good for goodness' sake.

CHAPTER 2

The Value of Community

Sister Sledge Got It Right—"We Are Fam-i-ly"

URING THE MID-'90s, I would frequently go to our local high school's baseball games. I would usually see and sit with the same group of guys at the games. One of the men often wore a "Promise Keepers" shirt. Another one of the regulars was very cynical about the Promise Keeper rallies, and the two engaged in much good-natured bantering about the organization. Promise Keepers, a Christian men's organization, was at its peak at this time, attracting large crowds for rallies at major football stadiums. These gatherings were a mix of pep rally, revival, and Amway distributor meetings. The cynical guy called them "sanctified Iron John meetings" for wimps and whiners who wanted to be holy.

"Iron John" was a reference to a secular men's movement, led by the poet Robert Bly, which was seen by some to have wandered off the beaten path. The cynic sarcastically said the only redeeming value in these meetings was that they cured people of unresolved gender issues. "If hugging a guy standing next to you while singing the '90s equivalent of 'Kum Ba Yah' and telling strange men that you loved them was repulsive, then you knew you were straight. If you liked it, then pack up your Village People tapes and move to San Francisco." His favorite line was, "Why would I attend one of these meetings? If I wanted to be with bunch of crazy people for a whole Saturday, I would go to my wife's family reunion."

On one occasion, one of the other men in the group suggested that Promise Keepers was just attempting to build a sense of community among men. Our witty friend replied, "The only time I ever participated in building community was during college when I worked on a construction crew building a state prison."

Several years later, a very popular high school baseball coach died in his early 50s. Our church hosted both the family's receiving of friends on the night prior to the funeral, as well as the formal memorial service. More than 2000 people, most of them of men, gathered to express condolences to the family. The most intriguing aspect of the evening occurred on the sidewalks and lawn of the church as people waited their turn to individually speak to the family. On this beautiful fall evening, the line moved slowly and men gathered in groups, told stories, laughed, cried, hugged, traded phone numbers and email addresses, and more importantly, started working through their grief.

My cynical friend, who earlier ridiculed the men's movement, told me how meaningful the family night been for him. He said, "When I arrived that night, I was not sure I would ever go to another high school baseball game. But even though I will not go to a game without remembering Coach, I am ready for the next season. It was good for me." Although he would never publicly acknowledge the need for building community, he was practicing community.

Community: A Low Priority?

Community is a virtue that has not been a priority for this generation of midlifers. Contributing to this low prioritization is the fact that community is one of the more difficult virtues to define. In most publications from 1950 to 1975, "community" referred to people gathered in one location and became a synonym for neighborhood, small town, or housing development. More recently, we have understood community to mean a group developed by people who hold some shared values in common. Many assume that Aristotle was the first to define this concept of community. Using this definition, a person can be a participating member in several communities simultaneously, and many of us would say that we do practice community through church, professional associations, and with neighbors.

Without finding a precise and technical definition, I find the best description of community as virtue is to recognize that I have an obligation to those with whom I have a common or shared set of values. To live in community is to actively engage with them as a duty rather than just as a means of using them for my purpose. Although community is not perceived as a vice by boomers, it is usually seen as one option among many, albeit a good option; if community occurs, good, and if not, oh well.

This is an issue larger than vocabulary, yet it can be illustrated through the way we use words. During the last 20 years, the word "team" was introduced into the common vocabulary of the workplace, and it happened on our watch. Yet many who teach the team concept will tell you that often people over 40 years of age will use the term without really understanding the concept. While we have professed to love team sports and have elevated college and professional athletics to an almost religious status, we have also dramatically changed team sports. Some would suggest that there are no longer any team sports; rather, there are events where athletes show up and play on the same fields or arenas with other athletes.

When baby boomers became the marquee players, the rules of team sports changed. Prior to this generation, most teams only had the names of the team and the player's numbers printed on their uniforms. But now, almost all teams have the last names of the individual players on the backs of their uniforms, regardless of whether they play on a professional team or in the local church over-40 softball league. In the past, the sports news featured the scores of the games; now scores are secondary to the individual highlights.

Free agency changed professional sports, giving individual players the right to choose teams rather teams choosing players. While free agency was presented as an economic or labor rights issue, it is also very much a cultural shift that is symptomatic of how we think about community and our responsibility to others. One well-known college coach said the first two questions high school seniors ask when he is recruiting them to play in his program are, "How much time will I get to play my freshman year?" and "Can you help get me ready for the pros?" He said frequently they fail to ask what kind of team will they have the next year.

> When baby boomers became the marquee players, the rules of team sports changed.

At the same time, baby boomers started a new phenomenon that is growing at an astounding rate. "Fantasy sports leagues" are a cottage industry. Using the Internet, imaginary teams are formed based on the statistics of individual players. A fantasy league player is not interested in the win-loss record of his favorite team but only in the statistics of his favorite players. This game is played primarily on the Internet by people who no longer look at the standing of the teams or know the real names of people who are in their fantasy league.

The shift from the emphasis on the team to accenting the achievements of the individual is not limited to sports and athletics. Even the arts have become infected with our hyper-individualism. Between 1965 and 1985, school and college choirs declined while small groups that were designed to allow one microphone per member began to be the preferred style of performance. The popular musical groups of the 1940s and 1950s were known by the group name and very few people ever knew the name individual musicians. But Ringo, John, Paul, and George changed that forever. Sports and music, often on opposite sides of the cultural divide, both moved in the same direction with the baby boomers. An art teacher in a community college observed that when middle-aged folks paint or sculpt in his class, they no longer find ways to hide their signature in their art but instead try to make sure that the viewer will know the creator.

Lone Ranger Religion

During this era, we saw the emergence of a "Lone Ranger religion." In the name of rejecting institutionalism, many chose to leave organized religion and to practice their faith individually without the burden of having to engage others. The country music song, "Me and Jesus Got Our Own Thing Going" resonated with many who were too cultured to acknowledge the validity of the music style. Yet in far more sophisticated ways, they expressed the sentiment themselves. Perhaps in his book *Habits of the Heart*, Robert Bella's poignant description of Sheila, a nurse who developed a personalized faith based on her preferences called "Sheilaism," reflected a major movement away from the concept of community. Even our passion for larger churches often works against community in that large church members often go to watch the superstars on the platform while they sit with strangers in the pew to whom they sense no obligation.

However, God created us to be in community. It is impossible to be good and then violate one of the purposes of our creation. Both the Old Testament and the New Testament tell the stories of community and are written to the community of faith. Although the Old Testament is filled with the stories of heroic individuals, these are not isolated events of bravery and courage. These men and women acted in the context of the people of God. Leviticus and Numbers, two Old Testament books we do not like to read, are about community rules and guidelines. One of Jesus' first acts in His public ministry was to form a group who were accountable to Him and each other. We call the group the twelve disciples. After the resurrection and ascension, new Jesus groups formed, and most of the letters in the apostle Paul are directed to these communities called churches.

We were created to live in groups and to be responsible and accountable to them. This is not in lieu of being responsible to God but part of being responsible to God. Maybe of all the values needed to be good, community is the most difficult for this particular midlife generation. It's not that community goes against our nature, but it does run counter to our training. Community is often an acquired virtue for baby boomers because our individualist culture pulled us in a different direction during our formative years.

The first wave of baby boomers grew up hearing war heroes tell their stories. But the stories of World War II were not only about isolated acts of courage, but also about how people in a depressed economy forged into a community. For the first time in American history, we really functioned as "one nation under God." It was not uncommon for tales of these heroes to be used as story lines for movies and as illustrations at church.

At the same time, these young minds were being shaped by the westerns they watched on television. Although this form of television drama was short-lived, it made a deep imprint on the minds of the young viewers. Westerns usually involved one person saving the west from a bad group. It was the hero against the group. When these groups were not presented as villains, they were often portrayed as mindless masses who needed some hero to rescue them. One cowboy wearing a white hat, riding a black horse, traveling with an obviously mentally inferior sidekick helped the poor helpless residents live happily ever after.

The folks born after 1968 not only appreciate community, but they also intentionally create and build community.

The second wave of baby boomers arrived and thrived in the "me" generation. Students were told that joy was found in doing what you wanted. The eleventh commandment was "do your own thing." Ironically, Woodstock rock festival in New York in the late summer of 1969, a celebration honoring individuality, took on almost sacred proportions. Today's youth who read about this event interpret it as an example of massive community.

While Woodstock did acknowledge our need for community, its purpose was quite the opposite. This temporary city of over 500,000, welcoming all people and all behavior in the name of sex, drugs, and rock 'n' roll, was to be a moment in time where every person could be radically free from the restrictive rules of the establishment. It is important to note that "the establishment" is a form of community and to be anti-establishment is to pit one community against another. No wonder so many are community-challenged and confused. Woodstock, an anti-community event which has now taken on mythological proportions, allowed many new communities to form. The number of Web sites dedicated to Woodstock and blogs written by participants gives evidence that as much as community was minimized, it was needed.

The generations that followed the baby boomers understand community better than those of us who thought our generation was God's post-war gift to humanity. The folks born after 1968 not only appreciate community, they also intentionally create and build community. While baby boomers often saw small groups only as a means to an end, the Buster and Generation X crowds see small groups as having intrinsic value, value in themselves. These people gather at Starbucks and Barnes & Noble for no other greater purpose than to gather. The 40-something folks go to drink coffee and read while the younger folks go to hang out. Boomers find it difficult to shed our task-oriented skin; we want the group or community to accomplish something. Sometimes it is just about being there. And in process of being there, we take steps toward goodness.

Community Is a Faith-Based Virtue

Community is a faith-based virtue and is directly related to our Christian faith. Those folks whose souls tilt toward individualism often perceive building and creating community as a social virtue more than a religious issue. But those who do not value building community as an act of Christian obedience will make their spiritual journey a self-centered walk in which they invite God to walk with them. God becomes a means that helps us to accomplish our goals. Then, when we hit those seasons of life when we are not achieving our goals, we jettison God as excess baggage. But if loving is joining God's walk, and if that journey has always been in the context of a group, then joining with community is not just good, it is part of an authentic Christian faith. Jesus made it clear that if we love Him we will love His people.

Community is a value whose meaning can get lost in esoteric discussions. By using emotionally-laden words to describe it, community can sound like a support group for losers. Regardless, living in community is both a requirement and a choice—a requirement because God created us to be and live in community, and a choice when we intentionally seek to live in common unity with others. Community is much more than being in some good group relationship; it means that we accept some responsibility for the group and commit to working for the good of the group.

Relationship is different than community. Community is one particular type of multi-tiered relationship. One description of the difference between *community* and *relationship* that is occasionally used in team-building exercises is, "Community is how to connect to a group of several people at a time, and relationship is how you connect to people in the group individually." You can have good relationships without building community.

Community is rooted in the Christian faith and is one of the more persistent themes in Scripture. Most of the letters of the New Testament are addressed to specific churches or communities and deal with community issues. The Bible is a good place to begin to understand how to experience authentic community. Although I do not know that it has been validated by research, conventional wisdom says that baby boomers have bought more Bibles than any other generation while reading it less. Our parents often had a family Bible and then carried a Bible to church. In most homes today, there are several Bibles in several different translations.

The New Testament's Book of James is a letter written by the half-brother of Jesus to a community of believers. It is important to note that the sense of community they had was not the result of location. Many believe that James is writing to those who were forced to leave Jerusalem because of persecution and were scattered in several different geographical locations. In spite of being separated by distance and by some cultural differences, James writes to them as if they are one group, because they are.

James fully understands the good news of the faith, yet there is a harsh tone to his letter. He is concerned that those in the community think grace and faith have exempted them from their responsibility to others. He does not suggest but requires them to take care of the needy and neglected among them. Evidence of authentic religion is providing for the widow and orphans (James 1:27). Faith without works is dead, which means faith that does not involve connecting with community is really not faith.

The types of works that James refers to are not personal sexual morality or ceremonial activities. It is caring for and ministering to people in the faith community. James later chides them for giving preferential treatment to the rich and ignoring the poor in their community (James 2). Teachers are reminded that in the process of teaching truth they must be careful they do not hurt the group or the community by using hurtful words. The prayer of healing is even described as a community activity, which is much different than the wandering healers who were prominent in that part of the world in the first century, and still exist on twenty-first-century cable networks.

It's Not About You

Community is genuinely caring about others. It is not being in relationship with people or organizations that can help you. To have community as a value means you are interested in the well-being of your world, nation, city, and church. It also means you are willing to invest in making your neighborhood, church, city, nation, and world better.

During the reign of the baby boomers, we have seen a decline in participation in civic clubs and service organizations. The G.I. Joes came home from World War II and invested in their communities and civic organizations. But presently, many internationally-known civic and service organizations are declining and are seeking members with the intensity of a televangelist looking for a mailing list. One major civic organization is considering a major media campaign to entice professional women and men to join. Some Christians and a few religious organizations have even warned that community service is just "do goodism" and can get in the way of church activities. Others see civic organizations only to be of a value if you use it as a recruiting ground to secure more heads and coins for the Sunday nickel and nose count.

A large civic organization did some focus groups among younger folks to find out why they were not joining civic organizations. One of the surprising answers was that the civic clubs and service organizations were not perceived as places to interact or serve. A facilitator told me that once he received a note from a 28-year-old rising star attorney who asked, "Why would I want to sit and eat in silence at a table of middle-aged folks who only speak if they are complaining about increased club dues and federal taxes, and who leave early if the guest speaker does not tell them how to make money?" I've visited the club he was describing and he was right. The baby boomer in charge has turned the club into a weekly infomercial for the local chamber of commerce.

We sometimes make community events into a place for us to purchase information and relationships that will help us get ahead. Under these circumstances, community just becomes a means to an end rather an authentic gathering of people with a common bond. While service clubs have declined, special self-interest clubs have grown. Almost every major city has a growing "Quarterback Club" and "Tip-off Club" filled with middle-aged adults who hear coaches and players from their favorite teams tell of their latest exploits. Most of these clubs contribute to a charity as well, but often the amount contributed is embarrassingly small. The format of these meetings is simple: sit, eat, listen, and leave.

Although there is obviously nothing inherently wrong with participating in special interest clubs, very little community is experienced by hearing physically pampered athletes and over-paid coaches tell you what will make you feel good on Saturday or Sunday afternoon. A minority gentleman said that they had to pay college students to lead a mentoring program at the local middle school. He was convinced that the lack of community support was the direct result of not having an outstanding athlete come out of the city in the previous five years. In a moment of frustration he said, "People only care about the hurting children of our community if they can do something with a ball and then attend their alma maters; otherwise, it is as if we do not exist."

A major step toward community is recognizing that we do have a moral and spiritual responsibility not only to individuals but to groups and groupings of people. Practicing the virtue of community can help us make progress in some of the critical issues in our society. While we have made improvements in racial reconciliation in our country, we still have a long way to go. Legislation has removed some of the barriers that block community, but legislation cannot create community.

If You Build It

Five years ago our church built a great state-of-the-art recreation center and encouraged young adults and kids in some of the deprived areas of the city to participate. They came to the recreation center, participated, and went home. We congratulated ourselves for the good we had done. But we did not really see any progress regarding racial reconciliation in anyone's life until we had some sense of responsibility and began to develop community between the leaders and the participants.

Three members in particular did more than coach basketball; they became engaged in their players' lives. They would make sure these guys were showing up for work and checked on them when they were not feeling well. One mother called to thank me for the two young men from our church who had taken an interest in her 21-year-old son. She said, "These two men really care about us." Since that phone call, I have had the privilege of developing a friendship with her and her husband. The coaches' actions in building community allowed me to experience community.

Whether it is civic clubs, sports activities, or the arts, connect with the groups around you—not just as a means to change them, but because it is a way of being a good person. Midlife may provide many excuses to exit from group responsibility; however, it is not the time to walk away from the community duties God has created us to perform. It is a time to reinvest with new energy, not necessarily because these efforts will produce a better world, but because by doing so, you will be a better person.

This awareness is not limited to local recognition of need. As baby boomers control the culture, we are becoming more of a homeland conscience.

> *It is a time to reinvest with new energy, not necessarily because these efforts will produce a better world, but because by doing so, you will be a better person.*

No doubt the events of September 11, 2001, have escalated our interest in our borders, but our compassion radar doesn't reach as far as it did. The national news used to be the most-watched part of the programming the national networks produced. The national news shows no longer carry the advertising weight for the networks. In many areas, the local news pulls in much higher ratings than national news. Some radio and television stations eliminated national and international news altogether except in national emergencies. The media is clearly reacting to the move away from global concerns to local issues.

Community is more than identifying with our neighborhood. It is also about solidarity with other people. I do not know how, but I got on the mailing list of a ministry that creates awareness of persecuted Christians throughout the world. I consider myself a fairly compassionate person, but I really have not been concerned about these folks.

Then I took a mission trip and spent several days with a missionary who began telling me stories of the persecuted church in other countries. These were stories from the country in which he was serving, but other places far outside his domain of responsibility. He said, "A call to missions is more than about caring for Christians in one area; it is about loving all oppressed people." We will build stronger bonds of community when we allow our hearts to be broken for the broken people of this world.

Building the virtue of community may require you to listen to your news differently. Building community may require you to read something other than business, sports, and local sections in the newspapers. Community people are willing to realize that they are affected by or a part of what is happening around the world.

Recently Harvey Thomas, former press aide to Margaret Thatcher, was speaking to a religious gathering in Birmingham, Alabama. He was asked for his observations of America. Along with a genuine admiration for much that happens in our country, he confessed he was dismayed by Americans' ignorance of world events. Another observer of the social scene said, "Many middle-aged Americans have not read more than the headlines of any story about the plight of international refugees since they stopped getting a Weekly Reader in elementary school."

Taking Initiative

Another important step in developing community is taking initiative toward the hurting. Many of the humanitarian pleas for funding in the United States have involved media presentations of small children whose eyes and faces were pleading for money. These campaigns have been very effective, but they may have inadvertently programmed us to respond to begging rather than leading us to reach out to people before they beg.

There is nothing more degrading than begging. It is difficult for real community to develop between a beggar and an emotionally coerced donor. We increase the possibility that community can develop when we respond to observed needs rather than to requests. One of the salient points made in the very familiar story of the Good Samaritan is that the hero of the story was never asked to help. He took the initiative and made it happen.

When our three children were very small, my wife and I served in a church which had limited resources. We saved money to buy a station wagon, and within a month, a taxi driver lost control of his vehicle and totaled the new car. The taxi company lawyer found a legal loophole, and we had to pay for close to 25% of the cost of a new car. An anonymous gift was delivered to me by an attorney in the community, which covered our costs and also helped pay for the medical bill.

After several months, I discovered that the donor was not only a friend but also a member of a small group I was a part of. When I asked if he and his wife were the donors, he gave a weak denial. Under no circumstances would I have asked him for help, and if he offered help, I think, at that stage of life, my ego would not have allowed me to receive it, and it would have damaged the small group. But he did not wait for me to ask and he did not put me in an uncomfortable position. He saw a need and met it. Our friendship and our small group were not impacted. We build community when we see a need and meet it, rather than making people ask or beg. Community will in some ways require the sharing of some type of resources, whether it is prayer, fellowship, or money.

Because initiative is often considered the property of the young, midlifers often become passive. They watch television with a remote control, give money rather than time to charitable causes, and email rather phone because it requires less actual engagement. Community requires initiative and engagement. It is more than giving to the United Way and helping someone when we are called. It is seeing the needs of humanity and taking the initiative to do something about it. The person who wants to experience good for goodness' sake cannot be passive.

You Can't Hide

The third step for developing community may be the most difficult of all. Community requires that we make ourselves vulnerable to hurt and disappointment. By midlife, we've learned how to hide, dodge the bullets, or shoot first and therefore avoid the pain.

Very early in my ministry, I got involved in a domestic squabble between a husband and wife that was ruining the lives of their small children. The husband and wife, who would not speak to each other unless they were cursing, made my life miserable for about three weeks. Anonymous letters, phone calls from their friends, and even the guy with whom the woman was having an affair made their way into my office.

I was telling one of our church and city leaders the story of my woe. I was proudly telling him how I had matured and learned my lesson about getting involved. He said, "I fear you may have learned the wrong lesson. What you did was right, regardless of how it turns out, and you may have to do it better next time. But if you are thinking maturity will remove you from hurt, then you have an immature understanding of maturity. Maturity means moving forward even while you are hurting."

It is interesting to note that while community became less important for the majority of baby boomers, for one subset it became a passion. The popularity of 12-step groups grew dramatically while the culture was becoming increasingly individualistic. Simultaneously, there was increasing awareness that support groups were effective in providing emotionally healing. But unfortunately, community was seen as only a cure for emotional sickness rather than as a means of maintaining spiritual and mental health.

Since community is a spiritual issue, it does require some specific spiritual efforts. The fourth step to developing community is to pray for people, nations, and cultures other than your own. One midlife man, who I would say seriously seeks to be good, spoke to a group of young professionals in our community. This gentleman has completed a successful business career at 50, and now has become an appointed government official. Due to his position, he is required to make some unpopular decisions. Yet he appears to handle opposition with a sense of civility. Though baited and badgered by his opponents and the press, I have not known him to deliberately or accidentally demean those who disagree with him. In his remarks to the group, he mentioned that for several years he has prayed for specific troubled parts of the world and for individuals and groups of people who trouble him. He said he found that praying for them made him much less likely to say anything insensitive about them. Community involves prayer.

The virtue of community is more than joining; it is engaging the world around you in the way God has engaged you. The Christian faith is based on Jesus entering our world and engaging both individuals and groups. Jesus was not only the Master of relationships but also the Creator of community. Jesus did not live as a monk. He was the Master who hurt for the hurting, who touched the troubled and troublesome, and who healed by walking with the masses rather than waving a magic wand at their pain. Jesus engaged the institutions and groups of His world. When we intentionally develop communities with the people in our lives, we are living like Jesus lived. When we begin to live like Jesus, we are making progress on the journey toward goodness for goodness' sake.

The truth is you are part of several groups that have common values, and to experience community you need to acknowledge that you have a moral and spiritual obligation to them. If you do, you will make progress in becoming the good person God created you to be!

CHAPTER 3

The Value
of Relationships

Rodney King Got It Partly Right—
"Why Can't We All Just Get Along?"

RODNEY KING'S LIFE WAS FILLED with a series of tragedies, but one chapter of his life made its mark on the 1990s. On March 3, 1991, King was observed driving recklessly and accelerating to over 100 miles per hour in a residential section of Los Angeles. When finally stopped, King refused to follow police officers' directives, and the police subdued him with 50,000-volt Tasers, 56 blows with nightsticks, and numerous vicious kicks to the body. All this was done by three officers while 24 others watched. The beating was videotaped by a resident of the neighborhood and released to the media. The brutal nature of the beating and King's bruised and swollen face were seen by millions of people.

The three officers who inflicted the blows were indicted for assault and two with falsifying reports. In a 1992 trial, the three were acquitted and the city of Los Angeles erupted with riots. Many lives were lost, sections of Los Angeles were left in ashes, and a city and nation were divided. King, in a televised plea for peace, asked in a gentle, broken voice, "Can we get along here? Can we all get along?"

At first, his question became the occasion for much social commentary. Eventually the question he asked was reduced to a punch line for the late night shows, and now nearly 15 years later it can get a laugh in a television situation comedy.

But King's troubles did not end with the riots. He has been arrested several times for spousal abuse, filed for bankruptcy in spite of being awarded a $3.8 million settlement by the Los Angeles Police Department, and has spent time in drug rehab. His life has been defined by problem relationships.

Rodney King is not the only person whose life has been damaged by failed relationships. For most adults, their greatest pain is a direct result of broken relationships or lack of relationships. Every night in America far more adults between the ages of 40 and 60 go to bed hurting than go to bed hungry.

Relationships or Illusion?

An acquaintance, feeling the pain of passing 50 on the calendar and 230 on the scales, called and said he wanted to buy me lunch. In the phone conversation, he told me that he had personnel issues in his company. A key employee needed professional counseling and their firm would pay for it. He wanted me to bring a list of at least three qualified counselors and phone numbers. He was always a fun guy to visit and has a keen sense of humor, so I was looking forward to the lunch.

We did the perfunctory Q/A that men use as starters to conversation, such as, "How you doing?" and "How is your family?" and "Have you eaten here before?" After the standard answers of "fine," "fine," and "I think I ate here with my wife," he quickly gave a brief summary of the employee's problem, and it was soon evident that the employee not only needed a counselor but was going to need another job as well. But then my acquaintance said to me, "I am really lonely." I moved my chair back from the table and lowered my voice to sound masculine and professional, fearing what I was going to hear next. I was as surprised at the next line as I had been at the first. My friend said, "I recently came to a painful conclusion that I am great at using people but I am terrible at relationships."

I responded, "You could have fooled me. I see you as very good with people." He said, "Yes, I know how to get what I want out of people, just like I got you to bring the names of the counselors. I am good at that, but getting people to do what you want is not a true Christian virtue, is it? If I'm not mistaken, even we Episcopalians don't believe 'Blessed are the manipulators' is a beatitude, except in a motivational seminar."

In the next several minutes, he unpacked his guilt about being manipulative with people and laid it out on the table for me to see. Yet as I listened to his story, I realized that it had a mirror image to it. I saw some of myself in it as well. This is a midlife issue for many people. Perhaps it true more for men than women because men's career paths provide many opportunities to use people, which at the time seem like obligations. But as more women are entering the competitive professional market, they are learning how to cast the illusion of relationship.

One of the cynical clichés regarding climbing the corporate ladder is, "It is not who you know or what you know that will get you to the top, but what you know about who you know that will jumpstart your career." Of course this is an over simplification, yet there is validity to it. We often use people and the information we know about them to get to the top. The old "tickler" file that was prominent in past generations has become digitalized with the Contact section of Microsoft Outlook. We note by each person what button they like pushed and when it is most effective for us to push it.

The 40/60 window of years provides opportunities to create real and lasting relationships that are not developed for the sole purpose of networking. To establish meaningful relationships is not to disdain the practice of networking. This is not a plea to start a 12-step group for recovering networkers, because if we did that everyone would want to join. Networking is a necessary part of life; but networking is not the same as establishing relationships.

The Bible on Relationship

Healthy relationships are a sign of emotional health. Relationships are an end, not just a means. The ability to form and develop healthy relationships is a virtue.

The previous three statements all present *relationship* as a character issue. We were created to be in relationship with God and others. The Bible, the authoritative book for Christians, is about relationships.

Although the opening verses of Genesis tell us about the creation of the earth, sky, seas, and all of nature, the rest of the Bible is about God's relationship with humanity.

> *Every event in Genesis after day five of the creation narrative is a relationship story.*

Every event in Genesis after day five of the creation narrative is a relationship story. The male-female relationship is introduced with Adam and Eve, and we read how they made decisions as a couple that impacted their relationship with God and with each other. Soon we find out that their family relationship was more like the Sopranos than the Huxtables. Noah struggles with people in and outside of his family. Character studies of the Old Testament patriarchs give more attention to the relationship issues than to mystical experiences with God. The mystical encounters with God are by no means minimized, but every recorded encounter with God impacts human relationships. God wired us to be in relationship with Him and with others.

Both Old and New Testament characters find ways to give the illusion of relationship with God and with others. Legalism is a substitute for authentic relationship. Rather than loving God with all their hearts, they attempted to just obey the rules without purpose or passion. Legalism changes how you perceive and understand God and others.

A legalist sees God as the great lawgiver and scorekeeper. He is not *person*, but *position*. Granted, it is an exalted position, but position is significantly less than the One who is person. The way you keep the lawgiver and scorekeeper off your back and out of your heart is to live by the rules and keep the law. Moses encountered God, and the law was a means of helping the people also encounter God. But the masses felt more comfortable trusting what was printed on the face of the stones than trusting the One who wrote on the face the stone. In the New Testament the critics of Jesus were bothered by the compassion that He had for the people and what they perceived as a lack of reverence for the rules. Their legalism kept them from seeing the face of God when they saw Jesus.

Legalism will also change the way you see other people. A legalist places people in one of two categories. They are either law keepers or lawbreakers. If they are law keepers, we praise them and emulate them. If they are lawbreakers, we condemn them and correct them. Even if we smile and act like we care while we are praising or condemning, it does not make these relationships healthy. Too often we place colleagues, friends, and even family members in one category or the other and interact accordingly.

Even without an awareness of the biblical foundation for relationships, observing human nature should establish the fact that we were created for relationship. It takes two people to create a third, and we identify that act of creation as a sexual relationship. An infant is not born and then abandoned, but is nurtured by parents. Children who are abandoned by their parents have difficulty functioning in life. Relationships are not the invention of a pop psychologist in California who appears on Oprah or Dr. Phil. Relationships were created by God, the maker of heaven and earth and all they who dwell therein. To avoid relationships is to avoid good character.

Relationships in Quantity

One of the more popular themes in western culture today is the need for community. Community is sometimes thought of as relationships in quantity. This is not only an inadequate understanding, it also diminishes the real meaning of relationships. The more we give people the opportunity to isolate themselves through technology, the more they want to gather in groups. But this trend does not mean that we are anxious to have relationships.

During the mid-'90s, while the shelf life of the Internet was still in doubt, a research group started a chat room and used it chart human behavior. They posted material—some tantalizing but not titillating information. Within several weeks the number of people interacting exceeded expectations. The researchers wanted to see what kind of people used chat rooms, so they suggested that they could meet in a location in a major city one specific Saturday afternoon. Because the chat room attracted people from all over North America, they expected maybe at most 25 people. Nearly 200 people showed up and many more wanted to set more meetings so they could attend. One of the researchers commented that though the meeting involved much conversation, he didn't think it was as much about relationships as it was that they just didn't want to be alone. When in search of goodness, the desire for relationships needs to be more than an escape from loneliness.

Relationships require openness and desire to be known. Our culture is learning the best place to have anonymity and to avoid being known is in a crowd. I attended the Taste of Chicago in Grant Park on a Sunday afternoon, along with some 25,000 people. I probably personally and literally bumped into several hundred people but said less than ten words in the two hours I was there. I did hear two ladies on the trolley as we were leaving discussing their day at the event. One lady said that she did not plan ever to attend again because it was hot, crowded, and all the food smelled like barbecue. The other lady said, "I loved it. You know I love being with people even when I do not know them. I am by nature a people-person. I just love to watch them." Maybe "voyeur" would a more accurate description of her than "people person."

At the same event, as I entered I observed two couples in their mid to late 40s seated on the ground underneath the shade of a tree. I assumed they were taking a brief respite from the heat. Two hours later, as I left I noticed them at the same location. Intrigued that they had not moved, I found a discreet place to stand and watch them. I could not hear, nor did I want to hear their conversation. Although there never appeared to a break in conversation, these four did not appear to be angry. Neither couple nor either sex appeared to be in charge. It looked like four equals in relationship. There were many young ladies present who were revealing their God-given and plastic surgeon-refined attributes, and little did they realize that what they were looking for was what the two couples under the tree had already found.

Relationships Are Difficult

But if you are created to be in relationship, then why are relationships so difficult to develop, maintain, and grow? Good relationships do cut across the grain to our selfish and self-centered nature. That is why authentic relationships have a spiritual foundation.

Left to our own devices and without guidance, we will destroy ourselves. Children will choose fast food, sugar coated anything, and caffeinated colas over healthy foods unless trained to do otherwise. Often adults have to be threatened by their physician, spouse, and government before they will give up destructive habits like smoking and overeating. While the U.S. government is correctly attempting to make sure no one starves to death, a large portion of our government health resources are directed to educate and train the rest of us not to eat ourselves to death. Why do we overeat? Because it requires less discipline and less effort than it does to eat properly.

Why do we avoid authentic relationships? Because it requires less discipline to avoid relationships or establish surface relationship than it does to develop right relationships. Relationships are work. Of course, that is why you were afraid of it, but it is true.

Over the past several months, there have been a number of articles about Generation X folks who have a deep sense of entitlement, believing their education and skills guarantee them the right to Enron executive-level salaries, tenured college professors' job security, and an MTV dress code. Yet this same generation appears to work harder at maintaining relationships than the baby boomers and busters. The present occupants of the 40/60 window were willing to work late hours, skip vacations, and send regrets to family functions in order to climb the ladder or make an additional contribution to their 401K. But relationships were seen as too much trouble to maintain because relationships complicated the relocations that climbing the career track required. You did not want to invest too much time, energy, or effort into people whom you might have to step on when reaching for the next rung of the ladder.

> *Relationships are a Christian value and a required core value of authentic goodness.*

Relationships do require work! But the good news is you can do it. Where do you start, other than just a promise to yourself to work harder?

It first begins with recognizing that relationships are a Christian value and a required core value of authentic goodness. If you see relationships as just a way to avoid the pain of loneliness, all attempts to motivate yourself will have as much impact as lectures on chastity did to Brittany Spears. It may require you to rethink faith issues and come to a better understanding of the God in the Bible. Seeing God as Father rather than rule maker is not only a good first step, it is consistent with Scripture. Remember when Jesus taught His disciples to pray? He encouraged them to use the term "abba," which is not the formal word a child would use when describing his most immediate ancestor, but the word a loved child would use when addressing his father in the privacy of the family.

Good Relationships Are Intentional

Although friendships are often formed accidentally, good relationships are almost always intentional. This is especially true at midlife. When our children are young, most of our friendships developed through our children. By attending tee ball games, piano recitals, ballet rehearsals, soccer practice, swim meets, and scouts, our lives intersect with other adults of similar age who are doing the parenting routine as well. If we get in the car pool routine, we hear of these families' ambitions and woes. The 20-minute journey to and from school often has the same conversation menu as last evening's meal. We know about the health condition of every member of these car pool families as well as we know our own.

But when our youngest child gets a driver's license, we enter the first rite of passage into midlife. When that youngest child graduates from high school, we are walking on the tightrope between being young and middle aged, and no one ever walks backward on that tightrope. The parents of our children's playmates have become our adult playmates, but we are no longer connected to them through our children. We occasionally run into them at social gatherings and we ask how their kids are and they ask how our kids are, and we have forgotten if and where they went to school just like they did about ours. After you get in the car, you say to your spouse, "They sure didn't have much to say," and you realize that neither did either of you. You ride home in silence, realizing that if you died they might have to hire pallbearers from a local temporary employment agency.

But if you need to have quality relationships in order to be a good person, where do you start? If you go back to the soccer fields or ballet recitals, they will think you are some out-of-town grandparents. You can't turn in a request to your church's intercessory prayer ministry that says, "Please pray that I will have a relationship with one person in addition to Jesus and my wife." This is, however, a good way to never have to do childcare duty at church, because you will not have the references to pass your church's child protection policy. Standing at a busy intersection with a "Will work for relationship" sign will get plenty of lookers, few takers, and numerous abusers. But seriously, where do you start without embarrassing yourself?

The best place to begin is with the people you already know. There are many people in your life who are at the acquaintance level. You have kept them there because you did not have the time or the interest in investing more in them. You may not even like them; it's not because you dislike them, it's because you really have never discovered anything in common with them. Their kid may have been on the other team, they may have attended that other church, they may have lived in that other neighborhood, or for whatever reason when you did meet them you didn't click and the magic didn't happen. But this isn't marriage and it is not even dating, so forget the chemistry stuff.

> *Standing at an intersection with a "Will work for relationship" sign will get plenty of lookers, few takers, and numerous abusers.*

A couple of years ago, a man I have known for ten years called and asked if we could go to lunch. I quickly agreed, thinking he may have seen the light and wanted to join the church I serve as pastor, or maybe he wanted my input in his life. We did the male small talk thing and then he said, "You probably want to know why I requested lunch." I did, but I played the game with a poker face. He said, "I would just like to get to know you. I don't want to be your best friend, but maybe a couple of times a year we could just have a conversation. We live in different worlds, but I would like for your world to have some influence in my world. Let me begin by telling you about my family and the challenges I am having in life, and then you can do the same if you like." In five minutes he gave me the male version of the family, facts without feelings, and a quick description of the next career mountain he is about to climb, and then I did the same. We still do this about twice a year and occasionally exchange emails. Two of my daughters were married in consecutive years, and each time this man left a message on my work phone at about the time of the wedding, wishing my family and me well on this special occasion. Although we do not see each other frequently, we do work to clear our calendars and stay up with each other.

I have since started the same pattern with two other men I have known, but with whom I did not have a relationship. One of these men is part of the G.I. Joe generation that made life easy for me, and the other is one of those busters who will be paying my social security for me. To be honest, I met with one of these men about twice, and it was evident that we had met at least once and maybe twice too often. The other man pushes me to think differently, and I encourage him to be right for a change, but we are good for each other. Granted, this is the male example of this, but women do this often and with more words and feelings.

I was in a community leadership group that met monthly over a year. I told this story to my small group, thinking I had discovered the elixir for middle age. A lady in the group told me she had always been in awe of another lady in the community and to some extent been intimidated by the way she always appeared to have life together. She was thin, looked good without make-up, never appeared to perspire, and her kids didn't have to wear braces. She was good. But the lady in my group said that when she turned 45, she called the lady without flaws and told her she admired her and wanted to meet her someday. Much to her amazement, Mrs. Perfect invited her over the very next day and the pair visited for two hours. A friendship began that has been going on for four years.

It's Not Brain Surgery

This sounds simplistic, but relationships are not like performing brain surgery. They are more like engaging in the process of growing up. In moments of reflection, most adults will look back at their young adult years and realize they were in a fog for long periods of time, just going where circumstances pushed them rather than making choices. Even the choices they did make were either driven by hormones or by someone else's expectations, rather than rational acts of will. Brain surgeons learn a skill, but maturity is more about awareness than skill. This is an additional reason that relationships are spiritual in nature. A good description of spirituality is the awareness of the power of the non-material. Christian spirituality is the awareness that through Jesus Christ the power of God in the person of the Holy Spirit is present and anxious to guide us in the choices we make. If God is the God that invites and calls us into relationship with Him and with His people, surely we can assume that God will guide us as we form new and healthy relationships.

For us to have good relationships, we not only have to be flexible, but the relationship needs to be flexible. Given today's political correctness debate, using "flexible" to describe people and values is often portrayed as a vice. If flexible means to have no core values and a willingness to adjust to all belief systems, then it is not virtue. But taking the word at face value, it means to be bent without injury or damage. When Christians are in relationship, they are not clones. They are people created in the image of God and with different spiritual gifts. Each is a unique creation at birth and a unique creation at new birth.

Walter is a frustrated and fearful man. If you observed him, you would think he is Christian leadership material. He keeps all the rules, attends church faithfully, and has led several moral-related campaigns in his state. But there is another side that has kept him from being effective as a leader and has minimized his influence. He is rigid in his views and his practices. He uses a calculator to figure the tips he leaves on the table and the tithe he places in the offering plate because he says he never wants to cheat a server or the Lord he serves, though his children say he doesn't want to overpay either. He led a campaign against a pastor who tried to add a worship service that had different music. He declined to vote in one presidential election because his preferred candidate

> *If God is the God that invites and calls us into relationship with Him and with His people, surely we can assume that God will guide us as we form new and healthy relationships.*

reversed sides on one issue. I met him one time. He quickly told me that he, like Lincoln, lived by the principle that he would rather be right than be popular, but I sensed his real governing principle was that he would rather be unpopular than change.

Although this fellow feels that he lives by the Ten Commandments, I see little evidence that he lives by the Sermon on the Mount. The Sermon on the Mount oozes with calls to be flexible without damaging or injuring your value system. The Sermon on the Mount does not contradict the Ten Commandments but expands into inner character issues that legalism works diligently to ignore. Living by the commandments is not the goal that good people take as their benchmark. It is the life of Jesus that is the standard by which we measure ourselves. The Sermon on the Mount is prophecy at it best because Jesus was not only proclaiming what kind of life we should live, He was also foretelling what kind of life He would live.

Boundaries and Blessings

Good character requires that we have relationships that have boundaries and blessings. Henry Cloud and John Townsend's wonderful books and seminars have brought a freedom to many people who lived as slaves in unhealthy relationships. Committing to a life of serving Christ does not mean you allow anyone and everyone to step on you like you are the sidewalk leading into a Wal-Mart on the day after Thanksgiving. Boundaries are not established only to help us to say "no," but also to help us know what to say "yes" to. If you say yes to everything, it is not long until a yes is not a productive answer to a person needing help. It is just another word they have heard before and yet have seen no results. Boundaries do not form our identity; instead they flow out of our identity.

People who have good relationships need to have a good self definition. This is why some people at midlife have few or no meaningful relationships. In the climbing process of their 20s and 30s, they became what everyone wanted them to be. They became the achiever at work, the caregiver at home, the committee chairperson at church, and the aging mother's rescuing child. Without an identity, they do not know where to start this relationship journey because their only identity has been in meeting other people's expectations.

A couple of years ago the church I serve as pastor asked a man who had shown great leadership ability in the three years he had been a member to assume a position of leadership. I, along with the church nominating committee, knew exactly why we needed him in this position at this particular stage of our church's life. When I met with him and shared with him the opportunity, he quickly and firmly declined. I told him that before he gave us a final answer I hoped he would think and pray about it. He told me that was unnecessary; the answer was unequivocally "no." He went ahead to say, "You and the nominating committee do not know me; you know what I have done and am doing, but you don't know me. My identity is another ministry in this church and I am convinced that God has created me, equipped me, and called me to this other ministry. If I say yes to this position, I will need to say no to my calling." He smiled and said, "Are we still friends?" He knew how to say no because he was aware of what he wanted to say yes to.

But if you set boundaries to help you say yes to what you need to do, you also have to bless the boundaries of others. Giving the blessing is key in developing good relationships and the best example of it is found in God. God blesses, not based on the quality of performance, but because we are made in His image. If the blessing of God could only be secured when we were good, then we always will feel unblessed. Many people have this image of God and as a result are always feeling inadequate, without worth, and victimized by life. They live out their victimization by making sure they are a victim through poor choices.

But God validates us for who we are, not what we do. Goodness and self-awareness go hand in hand in the Christian faith. Jesus did not call us to violate who we are but to claim who we are in Him. Who are we? We are created in His image, filled with His Spirit, called by His name, uniquely gifted by Him, and led to be in relationship with His people. But if that is who we are, then other believers have a similar identity. We must recognize that others need to establish boundaries as well.

Learning to Listen

As we age, we assume that we understand the life experiences of others. At about 40, we do not think we know everything, but we believe we have been exposed to everything. Every parent knows how obnoxious a 16-year-old can be when he finds his voice and believes he has found the mother lode of all wisdom. The teenager assumes that what he knows and is feeling no one else has ever known or felt accurately, and as a result comes across a know-it-all. A similar but not identical phenomenon can occur in midlife, which some have labeled as life's "second adolescence." The midlifer does not claim to know everything, but he does think he knows what most people want or feel. He has learned through several verbal spankings to not always reveal how confident he is about what others want or feel. He may keep his opinions to himself, but he responds to you as if he knows your needs, feelings, and greatest desires.

Eva is in her mid-40s and her youngest child has gone to college. Eva confides in her best friend, Marla, that she has a loss of energy and she wakes up in the night with very sad feelings. Marla recognizes these as symptoms of a person dealing with the empty nest syndrome. These two women have known each other since their children were small. They have attended the same church, passed around the same Dobson tape on childrearing, and signed the same petitions regarding pornographic magazines at convenience stores. Marla encourages Eva to find some new interests and assures her how great it is to have time to live out her dreams and have some romantic, uninterrupted evenings alone with her husband.

But Eva withdraws from Marla, who assumes Eva is now in the early stages of mild depression. Marla calls their pastor and Eva's husband to suggest that these two need to intervene and help Eva seek professional help. What Marla does not know is that Eva is dealing with guilt over her own college years and has been getting professional help for the last six months. Eva's college career gave no evidence that she would become the poster mother for a Focus on the Family. Attractive, insecure, and needing attention from males, she had many one-night stands. In her own words, "One fraternity passed me around like I was used furniture." Eva tells Marla to give her space, but Marla knows the problem is that Eva has too much space since the children are gone. The relationship is strained. Can this relationship be saved?

Although this situation was complicated, much of the difficulty was the result of Marla thinking that she understood it all. In our first adolescence we assume we know what no one else knows. In our second adolescence we assume we know what everyone feels and needs. Both stages of adolescence can make relationships difficult. At midlife we feel that we have so many experiences that we could write a book. Instead of writing our compiled wisdom, we speak it to those we love the most, but who usually already know it.

A Chicago Tribune columnist began a column with these words: "At a dinner party Friday night, I found myself listening to a rude, bombastic know-it-all who insisted upon lecturing the other attendees. Unfortunately, the know-it-all was me. I was hip-deep in my own fevered political rant before it occurred to me that my tablemates were intelligent, well-informed citizens who surely harbored their own opinions, hence I had better pipe down and—here was the towering challenge—listen to what someone else had to say" (Julia Keller, *Chicago Tribune*, June 27, 2005). In order to bless, we need to listen. Listening is not only a means of gathering information, it is the way we acknowledge that the speaker has worth and value. The people with whom you have a good relationship are probably those who have listened to you. It was not important whether or not they could repeat back to you verbatim what you said, but the value was that they validated you by listening. This takes us back to the beginning of the chapter. Listening is work, and relationships require work.

CHAPTER 4

The Value
of Personal Discipline

Barney Fife Got It Right—"Nip It in the Bud"

O NE OF THE MORE FAMOUS LINES spoken by Barney Fife on the *Andy Griffith Show* was "Nip it—nip it in the bud." Barney's advice is magic medicine that keeps bad actions from becoming destructive habits. But how do you stop "it" when "it" is no longer in the bud, but in full bloom? By the time the waters of time have reached the 40-year mark, many of the occasional bad actions associated with youth have worked themselves well beneath the veneer of our lives and have become habits. Breaking habits that are now well-established patterns can be more difficult for midlifers than for a college sophomore. Yet the antidote for bad actions, regardless of age, is self-discipline.

Paul Simon, in his powerful *Graceland* album of the '80s, asked this question: "Why am I so soft in the middle? The rest of my life is so hard." The most common demon of midlife may be the lack of discipline. Although a person in midlife may have a reservoir of wisdom and experience, the reserves of willpower are often running low. The examples of loss of willpower are legion.

A man sits in front of the big screen television night after night with a remote in his hand and runs through the channels as if he were playing a video game. He knows that he is really not watching any of the programming and should go to bed and get some rest. Yet he does not have the willpower to stop the channel surfing or the energy to go to bed. He falls asleep sprawled out in the recliner while his wife goes to bed humming the country music tune popular when she was in her 20s, "Lonely Women Make Good Lovers."

A midlife lady tells herself daily that this is the first day of the rest of her thin life. She leaves the house with every intention of following the Weight Watchers numerical count at lunch and concluding the day at the gym. Instead of counting calories at lunch, she meets her noonday regulars at the sidewalk café. While sipping her latté and dividing a dessert with friends, she comments on the number of under-clad twenty-something women who are running on their lunch hour. She says that someone needs to tell these nearly naked runners that they need to wear more clothes, while the runners look at her group and think someone needs to tell them to exercise. The reason they do not exercise is lack of self-discipline.

A couple in their 40s who religiously attended church when their children were small now participate occasionally but never miss when their college students are home on the weekends. At one time, parents of college students were fearful that their children would not attend church while away at the university. Now there is some informal research that suggests that the church attendance patterns of empty nesters are very similar to that of college students. The reasons adults give for not participating in the life of the community of faith sounds similar to the responses an undisciplined 19-year-old would give.

The Second Adolescence

Why, after all of these years of stressing the value of self-discipline to their children, do these same adults default to undisciplined patterns of living? If the senior adult stage of life can be called the second childhood, then perhaps midlife should be called the second adolescence. The first adolescence was not easy, and the second is no less difficult. One reason the first adolescence is so difficult is because purpose or direction is unclear. Middle school students are attempting to determine who they are at an age and stage of life that is confusing. The urges of the body do not match our circumstances. Adolescents don't feel comfortable in the skin of a child or in the body of an adult; yet some days they have the biological urges of an adult body and the fragility of a child.

As they enter high school, the significant adults in their lives tell them they need to be making decisions that will prepare them for college and beyond. Yet young adulthood seems to be light years away, and instead they want to make decisions that will help them feel accepted and loved now. While adults encourage them to develop character, the guys are noticing the girls, and the girls are hoping that the flirting will develop into a relationship. Children like to be asked, "What are you going to be when you grow up?" because the question allows them to use their imagination. Eighteen-year-olds will answer that question quickly because they have usually spent their senior year in high school attempting to find two or three plausible life maps. But middle-schoolers frequently despise this question because they do not have a clue what the answer is, and if they do, they feel powerless to make their wish a reality.

> *What are you going to be when you grow up?*

Fast forward some 30 years. Role and character confusion continue to exist. Women, who felt their options were limited because of childrearing or cultural expectations, often sense they are at a new stage in their life. They are not only unsure of what they are to be or do now that they are "all grown up," but even if they do have a direction, they often feel that the third and fourth decades of life primarily prepared them to be nurturers and caregivers. While failing to realize that nurturing may be the best laboratory for developing self-discipline, they feel inadequate. A 47-year-old mother of two college students told me after her first year of her graduate school, "I have learned that being organized is not the same as being self-disciplined. Organization helps you to do more, but to some extent it diminishes self-discipline because it gives you the time to give in to the expectations of others as well as your self-imposed demands." This lady explained that she was able to accomplish more each day than she ever expected, but she was not certain that most of it was either necessary or helpful.

A man who had made his living by using his palm pilot as his time and energy compass enters a new stage of life. No longer is he the "young buck" who needed to maximize every minute. At 50, he finds he is expected to be one of the corporate wise men. Instead of being the troubleshooter who discovers the flaws, he is the one the young employees come to needing someone to help them discover their own answers. This means that there are days that his Outlook calendar on the computer screen is not filled with appointments and reminders of phone calls to return. Using the practice putter his children gave him for Christmas is too obvious, so he plays computer games on the Internet. He says, "I am embarrassed to admit that I sit at my desk doing what I would chastise junior executives for doing. I don't know what to do when my agenda is not established by others." When he speaks of the need to reorient his life, he is describing the character issue of self-discipline.

Goodness Requires Discipline

Possessing or achieving the virtue of goodness requires self-discipline. It is tempting to assume that self-discipline is the sum total of goodness, but goodness exceeds self-discipline. Self-discipline is not a substitute for community or relationships. Some people who commit the worst acts may be better disciplined than those who do good deeds.

In 2005, many residents of Wichita, Kansas, were shocked when the feared BTK serial murderer was arrested and convicted of killing several residents over the span of a quarter of a century. When Dennis Rader was arrested, his acquaintances were in a state of unbelief. They described him as a very disciplined man. In the weeks that followed his chilling detailed confession of his destructive acts in court, the media interviewed several experts who had studied the patterns of serial killers. All of the criminologists I heard commented that Dennis Rader's self-discipline was what kept him from being detected for so many years. Most of the murders were committed before he reached of the age of 40. When he was discovered in his mid-50s, his careless inattention to detail was one factor that led to his being apprehended. His practice of self-discipline contributed to his evil, and his lack of self-discipline led to Wichita, Kansas, becoming a safer community. Self-discipline is not synonymous with goodness; yet to reach goodness, you can never stray far from self-discipline.

The beginning of self-discipline is understanding the first word, "self." If you do not understand who you are and what your purpose in life is, discipline will be just one more issue that adds to the confusion of life. Rick Warren's book *The Purpose Driven Life* addresses this issue as well as any recent publication. "It is not about you" has become the mantra of those who have really comprehended Warren's primary concept. Self-discipline that begins with the assumption that life is about meeting and fulfilling your desires will help an individual do more. But doing more does not necessarily lead to the destination of goodness. Knowing that the purpose of life is "to glorify God, and to enjoy Him forever" is where self-discipline begins. *What do I need to do or need to stop doing that will help me glorify God?* is the question as we seek the goodness attribute of self-discipline.

Purpose or Function

It is tempting to confuse our purpose in life with our function in life. The singular purpose as stated earlier is to glorify God, but there are many different ways or means of doing this. While many men and women assume that the primary way they find their purpose is through what they do for living, at about midlife there is often a growing awareness that what you do for a living has very little to do with glorifying God and more to do with meeting material needs, being driven by ambition, and acquiring marketable skills sets. As a result, many midlifers switch careers, thinking if they change what they do or where they work, they will find goodness. They may even give up tenured positions, good benefits, and high salaries, believing that they are purchasing salve for their troubled souls. Yet the new profession or the new position soon loses its allure, and they have the same depressing feelings and low energy level they had back when they were in their old positions.

Some seek to find their purpose in their marital status or their family. Many have felt that they could discover the meaning of life if they could either get married or become single again. Several years ago, a woman in her late 40s with four children explained to her community on a local talk radio show the reason she divorced her husband when the last child graduated from high school. She said she did it because "marriage was never my thing." She became a chronic composer of letters to the editor in a major city, and her writing suggested that many community practices and attitudes were also not "her thing." Others have married believing that the path to goodness would appear once they lifted the wedding veil.

All authentic self-discipline is faith based.

With all the forces of living moving against the need for self-discipline, where do you start? All authentic self-discipline is faith based. Knowing that your purpose in life is to glorify God and to enjoy Him forever provides the motivation for self-discipline. Self-discipline that fails to acknowledge that our purpose is to glorify God will always be temporary. How do we say "yes" to pain, inconvenience, and the delayed gratification we know feels so good and is as close as giving into our desires? We can say "no" to destructive desires and "yes" to discipline when we acknowledge that life is more than our "three score and ten" and that our time on this is earth is one small chapter in the context of the longer book called eternity.

The Christian faith does more than simply place the burden on our shoulders of glorifying some demanding all-powerful deity who is going annihilate us if he catches us not glorifying him. We are taught that the God who wants us to glorify Him loves us more than we love ourselves and desires more and better for us than we can even imagine for ourselves. To think that our purpose in life is to glorify a sovereign deity can be anything but appealing. But when we recognize that the God revealed in the Bible and through Jesus Christ is loving and merciful as well as all powerful, the burden changes into a blessing. For most, the key question is not, "Is there a God?" but "What is God like?" Although atheists often receive significant press in a secular culture, there are very few pure atheists. Some may question if there are any, but let's leave that question to theologians. It is sufficient to say there are few.

A fictional story, circulated several years ago and a staple in the repertoire of religious speakers, illustrates the paucity of atheists. A young man who had been reared in a religious home went away to college. He came home in the summer following his freshman year and told his devout and pious mother that although he was appreciative of her intentions, he no longer believed in religion and was an atheist. With a kind and gentle expression on her face, she looked at her son and said, "I don't believe a word of that; of course you believe in God." He said, "Mother, I have examined the facts and the supernatural is an imaginary crutch people have relied on for centuries to explain what was once unexplainable." The saintly lady looked at him and said, "Son, of course you believe in God. I remember when you said your prayers and read your Bible daily and never missed attending Sunday school." He countered, "I did that because it was what you taught me and these actions were for the purpose of obeying you and not authentic evidence of faith." She just smiled and said, "Of course you believe in God." Frustrated that his mother did not accept his atheism, he said, "I swear to God, I am atheist." She replied, "Thank you for making my point."

Understanding your purpose in life is more than believing in God. The Scripture teaches that even the demons believe and tremble. Organizing your life around the purpose for which you were created begins with knowing the kind of God you believe in. If your purpose is to glorify a scorekeeping God, you may cease some bad habits and start good ones, but it will be out of fear. Healthy self-discipline is more than doing right; it is choosing right for the right reasons.

Accountability

Establishing discipline in midlife is also directly related to accountability. During the last portion of the 20th century, accountability has become an "in" concept among men's groups. From Robert Bly's fans to McCartney's Promise Keepers, accountability, while often described in different terms, has called for guys to be honest with guys in small groups. Yet, while meeting in small groups and doing the "didja" routine, asking each other if they did the bad things and did the good things, they often found they could lie to other men as well as they did to their wives. While the language of accountability increased, there is little evidence that much accountability actually occurred. There has not been a rash of fidelity, a decrease in pornography, or an unexplained outbreak of ethical behavior among evangelical businessmen. The use of the "accountability" vocabulary appears to have inoculated many Christians against authentic accountability.

While accountability language does not appear to have invaded women's literature to the extent it did men's, much of the support group movement that has attracted women encourages a similar concept. Neither designating an accountability partner nor joining a support group with other women who carry the same cross as you do will automatically bring self-discipline.

The first step toward meaningful accountability generally begins with an attitude change. Baby boomers have drunk deeply from the world of individuality. Many believed that what they did, said, or thought was no one else's business if it did not hurt anyone. Many of the issues that fueled the social revolution of the 1960s, 1970s, and early 1980s were rooted in the belief that "no one needs to know." When baby boomers entered the work force, we first began to hear that certain questions were off limits in the interview process. Information like marital status, medical history, and weight, which had been on every application for earlier generations, began to disappear. Then, as baby boomers became supervisors and began to design employment application forms, questions of age, race, and education began to be eliminated. "Don't ask, don't tell" not only became a phrase that helped a president, but also entered the military vocabulary. Even churches and religious organizations sometimes used the biblical principal of the priesthood of the believer to mean "no one has a right to question my faith or my behavior."

> Accountability begins with the awareness that others do have a right to invade my moral space.

However, accountability begins with the awareness that others do have a right to invade my moral space. For some this is more than a mid-flight course correction; it is like changing planes at 30,000 feet while traveling at 500 miles per hour. To really believe that others not only have the right to ask questions but have the responsibility to examine and question our core values and our actions is completely alien to their understanding of life.

This concept of accountability is built on two Christian truths: the fallen nature of humanity and the Spirit of God dwelling in the faith community. If we do not think we are capable of doing wrong, we will question why we need to be examined. Or if we recognize our sinful condition but think that the convicting and comforting Spirit of God will reveal our sin directly to us without working through others, we will avoid situations and circumstances in which others can confront us.

A lady who led an interdenominational Bible study became quite angry with ladies in her group who questioned why she spent so much on clothes. With righteous indignation, she informed her interrogators that she tithed to her church and her husband was a well-paid professional. Further, she thought they needed to give more attention to the prophets of the Old Testament rather than to her personal profits. Ironically, she was teaching the Book of Amos when the questions were raised, and of course, Amos was a prophet who was very critical of the rich.

Accountability, although easier to talk than walk, is necessary for self-discipline. Virtue is not just avoiding bad behavior because we are afraid we are going to have to explain our actions to someone. It is deliberately doing the right thing because we know it is right. Healthy accountability is more than just answering questions. It is a moral dialogue with others that not only helps us avoid bad choices but also, and perhaps more importantly, provides opportunities to know right from wrong so that we can make the right choices.

Can We Change?

By midlife, not only have our daily routines become well established, but we also have our patterns of thinking so well encoded in our mental processes that we find it is difficult to change. A 54-year-old father of two and grandfather of three once asked me, "Can a man my age change my thinking habits without a lobotomy or brain tumor?" Although his question was tongue-in-check, the issue he addressed was real. Can adults change the way they think?

The answer is yes! Paul was not writing to the young or the novice when he penned these words in

Philippians 4:8: "Finally, brothers, whatever is true, whatever is noble, whatever is right, whatever is pure, whatever is lovely, whatever is admirable—if anything is excellent or praiseworthy—think about such things." While this verse has been frequently used as a memory verse for children, it was written to adults by an adult who was in midlife or just beyond it.

We can change not only our thoughts but also our pattern of thinking. Two tools that you can use are a thought journal and a thought map. A thought journal requires that you write down what you think about each day. Keep a thought pad on your desk and when you find yourself thinking negative and destructive thoughts, write down what you were thinking and if possible what triggered these thoughts. You do the same with the positive, wholesome, and beneficial thoughts you have during the day as well.

A friend of mine used this method to help him learn what he needed to avoid in order to change his pessimistic thinking. He discovered that when he was with two specific employees he became very negative in his thinking. One was a "bad news bearer," in that he was continually informing everyone of corporate problems, while the other employee frequently asked questions that led to self-doubt. It would not be wise or healthy for this corporate executive to always avoid these employees, but he did change when he met with them. He placed them before and after the employees who helped him think positively. The thought journal does not need to be detailed information regarding of our thoughts. It can be as simple as a one or two word summary of what we think about.

The lady who first introduced me to a thought journal was introduced to it herself during a peer review. During this review, she was informed that she was a negative person who spent more time looking for problems to solve than solving problems. One anonymous evaluation form suggested that she had become the coroner of the corporation rather than an organizational promoter. She then began a thought journal and was surprise to realize how much time and mental energy she gave to finding problems. She realized that she was not a problem solver but a problem identifier. The thought journal helped her become not only a better supervisor but also a person of better character.

A Thought Map

One proactive method of changing thought patterns is to do a thought map. Write down the things you want to think about and plan a time to think about them. This is more than writing down what you plan to do, but what you plan to think about.

A man who was going through a very painful divorce modeled this method for me. His wife divorced him and through deceit took most of their savings. She openly bragged about her husband's naiveté regarding divorce proceedings. He found that he frequently replayed the events and conversations that led up to the divorce on the screen of his mind. He said the index finger of his mind continually hit the rewind button. With the help of a friend, he made a list of the thoughts he wanted to think about each day.

He needed to give more attention to developing a strategy for the future than writing the memoirs of his failed marriage. He began with writing what he wanted to think about on his break, lunch hour, and in the evening. Later he developed a series of 3 x 5 cards that he placed on his desk to guide his wandering mind. It was a map for his thought patterns. He said in retrospect part of the reason his marriage failed was that he used too much energy early in the marriage thinking about the past rather than the future with his wife.

If we can control our thoughts, we have taken a major step toward controlling our feelings. Our minds and our emotions are very closely related. If we think the right thoughts, we will have the right feelings most of the time. During our youth we not only have many first time experiences but also have more first time thoughts. By the time we are 40, most experiences are either repeated or mutated forms of earlier experiences. As a result, when we encounter these identical or similar experiences, we pull up files from our emotional memory disc and click the replay icon.

For example, an acquaintance of mine told me how he emotionally responded to their monthly credit card bill. During the early years of the marriage, getting the credit card bill was usually a low-grade crisis. Each month he and his wife had to determine how they could scrape together enough money to pay the bill. In the process, they would analyze every expenditure, often for the purpose of blaming the other for the large bill. Now, 15 years later, this couple uses a credit card to pay for every purchase in order to avoid writing checks and carrying cash. Because their annual income is now close to a quarter of million dollars, they pay their bill in full each month and never pay any interest. Although lack of money is not an issue, he said that the same feelings emerge today when he opens their monthly credit card bill. He peruses each expenditure and always finds two or three to confront his wife with, questioning if the expenditures are really necessary. It is not unusual for them to have a conflict over less than $100. Recently, he realized the issue was not the money but his feelings. Feelings can get in circular ruts, and it takes self-discipline to break the cycle.

I have a colleague whose signature line has become "your feelings are not my responsibility." I first heard her use this statement when very kindly responding to an individual who was suggesting that she had unknowingly hurt his feelings. She apologized, but she also reminded the wounded fellow, who acknowledged that he was very sensitive,

> If we can control our thoughts, we have taken a major step toward controlling our feelings.

that she could not be responsible for every time he felt wounded. But if we are not responsible for each other's feelings, then who is? The definitive answer is: we are responsible for our own feelings. My colleague is right: My feelings are no one's responsibility but my own.

Avoid Self-Pity

In our culture we have made victimization an art form. While we have learned that often in the past we were insensitive to needs and hurts of others, we have also learned how to administer guilt on those who we think have been insensitive to us. It is the baby boomer generation that coined the phrase "out of my comfort zone" and brought it into our vocabulary as a legitimate excuse to avoid responsibility. A young lady who had recently been promoted to the role of supervisor caught an employee violating a corporate policy that was grounds for immediate dismissal. When she reported the incident and how she handled it to the regional vice president, she was asked why she did not dismiss the employee since the company could have some legal liability resulting from the violated policy. She said, "Although termination might be the right thing, I am not comfortable in firing anyone that I did not hire." In other words, I do not feel like doing what I know to be right.

The folks born between 1945 and 1965 are the first generation to have been reared in a litigation culture. We have seen the rewards of being a victim. The sense of entitlement that permeates our society may explain the contrasting demands for more government services and lower taxes that have to some extent kept several state and federal administrations in gridlock. Political liberals are the usual suspects, demanding more government services, while conservatives are quick to say they deserve to keep what they have earned. But the entitlement issue reaches far beyond politics and expands into emotional expectations. It is the feeling that every injustice needs to be acknowledged and rectified, and if the wronged one feels that no one is attempting to make it right, then the wronged one has the right to stay angry and to wear the crown of self-pity.

> *By the time we are 40, everyone with a good memory has enough experience to compose several "somebody done somebody wrong" songs.*

By the time we are 40, everyone with a good memory has enough experience to compose several "somebody done somebody wrong" songs. Rather than allowing these songs to be "elevator music" that continually run in our minds, the person of character must have the self-discipline to deliberately expunge feelings of self-pity. This may be the most difficult aspect of self-discipline to download into our daily experience. When we find ourselves feeling sorry for ourselves, we must realize that we are not just treading on dangerous ground, we are already in quicksand and the descent has started. Self-pity not only leads to sin; it is sin.

Without getting rid of self-pity there will be no meaningful self-discipline. Without self-discipline there will be no quality character and the prize of goodness will elude you. Here are some steps to overcoming the destructive and undisciplined path of self-pity or victimization.

• Begin and conclude each day with a time of thanksgiving. Let the virtue of thanksgiving be the first thought in your mind when you wake up and the last word out of your mouth before you go to sleep.

• Forgive the people who have wounded you in your past. If possible, tell them—not only does it empower the healing of a relationship, but also it helps hold you accountable. If it is impossible to express forgiveness to the person who has hurt you because of death, distance, or special circumstances, write a forgiveness letter and seal it. Then you may want to keep the sealed letter as a visual reminder of what you have forgiven.

> *Let the virtue of thanksgiving be the first thought in your mind when you wake up and the last word out of your mouth before you go to sleep.*

• In your daily quiet time, ask God to keep you from developing a bitter heart. One lady I know prays daily that she will forget her hurts and remember her blessings. During the publicity regarding the posting of the Ten Commandments, she had a desk ornament that read, "Do you know the 11th commandment?" When visitors in her office would ask what the 11th commandment was, she would reply, "Thou shalt get over it quickly."

• Keep a list of unexpected and undeserved breaks in life. Healthy individuals recognize that they can't blame their parents or children for the predicaments in which they find themselves. They know they must accept responsibility for their own feelings and actions. Yet this healthy stage also has a trap door. In the process, we assume that we are totally self-made individuals and forget that we have had breaks along the way. We did not choose to be born in the world's longest period of prosperity and in the age in which we have experienced greatest advances of health care. Although comparison is not always an effective way of reaching emotional health, we can set down and list the ways our life would have been different if we had been born 100 years earlier.

CHAPTER 5

The Value of Solitude

The Beatles Were on the Right Track
But Didn't Quite Get to the Station
When They Sang "Let It Be"

WHEN THE BEETLES RECORDED "LET IT BE," they developed a non-religious version of "Kum Ba Yah." The point of the song is to relax and let the world happen without getting too uptight about anything. While this was a refreshing word during the 1960s and 1970s, it does not lay tracks for the railroad car of life. If you totally "let it be," you won't "be" too long for this world.

In 1976, a young lady sat cross-legged on the median of a major traffic artery in Kansas City, Missouri, during rush hour traffic, holding a hand-painted sign. Her poster read, "Turn your radio off! Solitude brings serenity." On the evening local news telecast, a reporter interviewed this second semester freshman who was doing a project for a class at college. In the interview she stated that serenity was the key to life. She said that she was committed to lead a crusade for serenity. The fact that a life of serenity might exclude crusading for anything obviously had not crossed her mind, but it registered with the reporter. He ended the interview with the following words: "A crusade for serenity sounds to me like an oxymoron."

> By midlife, many have given up on serenity, but they would like to have some solitude.

By midlife, many have given up on serenity, but they would like to have some solitude. They hope that if they experience solitude often enough they may have some serendipitous experiences of serenity. Is solitude the property of only previous generations? Welcome to the interconnectedness of a midlifer.

A 47-year-old wife, mother, and grandmother recently described her Monday. On Sunday morning she made a commitment in a church service to develop a daily devotional life that would include prayer, Bible study, and reflection. Monday was to be her first attempt to incorporate the new spiritual regimen in her life. Before retiring on Sunday evening, she placed her Bible, notepad, and pencil on the kitchen table and set the timer on her coffee pot so she would have everything in place. If plan and intentions were guarantees of success, she would be the Donald Trump of spiritual wealth.

When the alarm sounded on Monday morning, her body argued with her soul for a couple of minutes. Her soul prevailed, so she got out of bed. The fragrance of fresh brewed coffee, combined with the visual of a Bible, note pad, and pen on the kitchen table gave her a hint of the feelings Neil Armstrong had when he landed on the moon. She thought, "One small step for my body, one giant step for my soul."

As she sat down, she received a call from her mother's nursing home to inform her that her mother was refusing to take her medicine. Although there was nothing she needed to do, the nursing home was required to notify her. She listened and said thank you. The phone awoke her husband and he came into the kitchen and wanted to know who called and why was she up so early. She explained about the call and that she was trying to do better in her spiritual walk. He said, "That's good," and then he went to the refrigerator, pulled out a Diet Coke, found a doughnut, and sat down at the kitchen table with her.

Normally she'd be delighted to have conversation with her husband, but not this morning. She did not want to tell him that she and God did not need him at this moment because she had already accumulated too much spiritual baggage. She started to read her Bible, while her husband, realizing he might be expected to do something religious, excused himself.

Next, the dog wanted out. So she got up from the table and opened the door to the backyard. As she sat back down again, the phone rang. It was her daughter who is away at college asking her to pick up a blouse she left at the cleaners the last time she was in town. Her daughter explained the reason she called so early was that she and two sorority sisters were up to do their early morning run.

Her husband yelled from the study that he could not open his email. He wanted to know if they have been having Internet problems. While he showered, she manipulated the computer and connected to the Internet. Then as she sat at the computer she checked her email and answered a few that required an immediate response. The last email to arrive informed her that the real estate clients she was to pick up at the airport at 10:00 A.M. are now arriving at 9:00 A.M., and in addition they have found another house on the Internet they want to see today. She gave up on the Monday morning quiet time and for a few minutes envied the sisters of silence at the Our Lady of Despair Convent.

The lady who told me this story said with a perplexed smile on her face, "And on Tuesday the pace really picked up."

Present day midlifers are not the first generation to have high demands on them, but they are the first generation to have the capability of being instantly connected with friends, family, work, marketers, and media. For the most part, few were prepared during either their formative years or during the professional training for what happened when they cut the ribbon on the information highway. An attorney who started with a major law firm in the late 1980s was taught during company orientation how to keep the phone and correspondence from controlling his time. But now at age 43, he is a prisoner of a Blackberry that his company provides for him. With this technology he can be reached by phone, email, or digital paging 24/7.

The issue is not whether constant connectedness is a permanent addition to our civilization or even if it is good for society in general. The issue facing us is:

how can a people live in a "plugged in" world without pulling the plug on their own soul?

Solitude and Goodness

Historically, solitude is considered one of the primary virtues associated with good character. Where do you start the journey toward healthy solitude? As a lady asked me on the week of her 40th birthday, "How do I get off of this bus called my life before it crashes?"

Solitude is not a virtue that you develop "cold turkey." The first step toward solitude is the precursor discipline of reflection. Character development requires reflection because authentic character requires that we not only know what is virtue and what is vice, but also know where we are on the continuum between the two. Continual connection to others and frenzied interactions with others make significant reflection impossible.

As result, some attempt to develop character by withdrawing while others assume that time management is the key that unlocks the door to character. While both contribute to the quality of life, neither automatically builds character. Solitude is a virtue when practiced properly, which leads to serenity. Authentic solitude is a character issue.

While both of these methods have helped a few people cope, more have found they are like the latest infomercial on weight loss. The best emotional reward was the first day they tried the "thin forever" potion advertised on late night cable. But, as Richard Foster says in his classic *Celebration of Discipline*, solitude is more a state of mind and heart than a place. Solitude is formed neither by the magic of withdrawal or by the acquiring of time management skills. Developing this state of mind and heart is a character issue, which means it is necessary if you want to become a good person. Withdrawing from the rat race often only means that we walk with the rats that no longer have the energy to run. Retreating, withdrawing, and pulling aside are terms that are used to describe attempts at solitude. Unfortunately, some choose to use these mechanisms as permanent ways to avoid responsibility.

Jesus provides the perfect example of deliberate and temporary withdrawal that allows for the refueling of the soul. Prior to the major events in the life of Jesus, the Gospel writers are careful to note that He withdrew or retreated to pray. The Gospel of John goes to great length to show Jesus preparing for the cross in the Garden of Gethsemane and asking the disciples to do likewise. Yet the disciples used the time to sleep rather than pray and reflect. We should not be surprised that on the day Jesus stayed focused on salvation, the disciples were interested only in survival. Solitude does help you survive, but if you see this virtue as a survival method you have to some extent already missed the point of the virtue.

Separation

Dale is a community and church leader who hit a major bump in the road near the age of 50. Even though his family-owned company is 1,000 miles away from New York City, his client base was bent out of shape by the events September 11, 2001. He had to make some hard decisions regarding downsizing and renegotiating loans. He did the right thing for the future of his company, but his decisions were not received well by his downsized employees. He hurt for and with his former employees. He was embarrassed because he knew their anger was known in the community.

Dale had enjoyed the respect and admiration that had come with a well-run family corporation. Dale met with his pastor and told him that due to his circumstances, he wanted to take a lower profile at the church. He also dropped out of a civic club and gave away his season tickets to the local college basketball games. He told his friends he was going to enjoy this opportunity to be less visible because he needed time to rethink his life issues and company strategies.

Yet he uses this time to brood. Instead of building character, he became a social hermit. While others in the same industry recovered in late 2003 and early 2004, neither he nor his company has. He will tell you that the reason for his present condition is still 9/11, but his opponents will say it was his 2003/2004 company strategy. The real issue may be that he has never developed the character discipline of solitude.

Dale separated without experiencing solitude. While the popular meaning of solitude is the quality or state of being alone or remote from society, the spiritual application of the word is more specific. Richard Foster says, "Loneliness is inner emptiness. Solitude is inner fulfillment." This description of solitude helps us understand why solitude can be experienced at any time even while we still may be connected to others.

Solitude is the spiritual awareness that God's presence with you is more important than the presence of or the absence of anything or anyone else. Solitude involves separation but is more than a geographical issue. It begins as a priority issue, and priorities are the direct result of reflection.

One summer I was stretched to my limits. Our church was finishing a building campaign, adding a new worship service, and ministering to several families with intense marriage problems. I decided to get away for a few days of study and reflection. I took my laptop computer, cell phone, and several books to read. I went to a hotel in a major city, since retreating to the woods rarely refills my creativity fuel cells.

The first day I spent returning phone calls and emails I had benignly neglected through the exercise of my gift of procrastination. On the second day I read books and worked on some detailed planning that required silence and no interruptions. After two days I felt good about what I had accomplished, but spiritually and emotionally I was still empty, perhaps even to a greater degree than when I had arrived.

On my third day I realized I had not disconnected from the things that were depleting my spirit. I was using technology to stay connected. I then determined not to view email, listen to voice mail, or work on projects on my laptop. While this did give me a feeling of righteousness, it was not the soul experience of solitude. The silence seemed to go on and on, and it seemed to be an empty silence.

In the boring silence, I began to think of the times in my life when I was aware of God's presence, leadership, and comfort. As I examined these encounters, I realized how ordinary the circumstances were. It was not that God did anything unusual but that I had chosen to be aware of God's presence. In a spiritual "aha," I recognized that what turned these ordinary events into meaningful experiences was my choice to be aware of God.

Often we blame our lack of solitude on schedules or that we have not had the wonderful retreat that all those super-spiritual people had. We have heard several Hollywood personalities who went away to some exotic location and found God.

> *In the boring silence, I began to think of the times in my life when I was aware of God's presence, leadership, and comfort.*

But they had the time to get away because their professional star was falling and they were now living off royalties. While our busy lives may contribute to the lack of solitude, that is not the only culprit. If Foster is right and we can experience solitude at any time, we also must acknowledge that our will is involved.

Can You Disconnect?

The first step for someone who does not experience solitude is often disconnecting, which is not the same as retreating or escaping. Disconnecting is not solitude; it is only a means to it.

The reason we do not disconnect daily is because we believe that what we are doing and experiencing is more important than anything else. Some midlifers wear their business duties as both their cross and their crown. It is the cross they bear when attempting to avoid responsibilities because they can always legitimately say they are too busy and people will believe them. In spite of honestly regretting their busy lives, on the inside of their souls they feel quite good about the amount of multitasking they do each day. They assume that they must have worth and value or they would not have so much to do.

Have we not heard of the danger of too little to do? Maybe those folks who warned us of the danger of sloth assumed we would innately know that business and connectedness were not the antonyms of sloth. In the name of good works, we have become busy pagans who have no space in our days for encounters with God.

Although this false concept of self-worth is a temptation for all ages, it may be more imminent and directly accessible at midlife. By their early 40s, many adults are realizing that their children no longer need them for survival. If we have done an adequate job of rearing our children, they should be able to live without us. But why don't they, then? Could it be we buy them cell phones not for their safety but because of our insecurity?

By midlife people in our companies and organizations are already preparing to take our place. It is a humbling moment to realize that people are already attempting to figure out who is going to replace you when you are gone. A 50-year-old father told me of the ambivalent feelings he had when he realized that although his children would miss him when he died, they could function very well without him and that the small company he had founded would open the day after his funeral and resume business as usual. So what do we do when we realize that we are mere mortals whose roles will be filled before our grave will be? We often fill our lives with things that give us feelings of worth.

Yet, for the follower of Jesus Christ, we recognize that authentic self-worth comes from our relationship with God. Solitude is the action of recognizing and experiencing that truth. It is difficult to acknowledge this when we are emotionally connected to routines that we have allowed to become the source of our worth. We stay connected for fear of losing our self-worth; and by staying connected, we do lose our self-worth. We are depressed if we do and depressed if we don't.

Addicted to an Illusion

Several years ago an acquaintance had high-risk surgery. During the surgery, he experienced severe complications. Following the surgery, he required an injection of a potent medicine every few hours for three days. The injection significantly improved his condition. After the first day he was fully conscious of what they were doing and when they were injecting the medicine. He became very anxious if he thought the hospital staffers were late with the injection or that they were reducing the amount of the dosage. The physician told him that after prolonged usage there were some long-term side effects of the medication. The patient told his team of physicians that he was more than willing to risk the potential side effects.

When his physician informed him that he had not had any of the medicine for 72 hours, he was angry.

Without telling the patient, the hospital staff gave a placebo on the seventh and eighth days. On the tenth day he told his physician that he did not believe he would live without the medication. When his physician informed him that he had not had any of the medicine for 72 hours, he was angry. But then he realized he had become emotionally addicted to an illusion. Business, activity, and connectedness are illusions that we mistakenly assume give us self-worth. After living with the illusion for several years, we mistakenly assume that we cannot live without them.

Another necessary step toward serenity is looking at why we are so connected to the people and tasks around us. Again, this requires reflection. Disconnection without reflection is simply being unattached to anything. It can make you feel like you are simply being blown by the wind without being anchored down. This may be one reason people fear the act of disconnecting from the demands made upon them. Below are seven questions that I have found help me turn disconnection into reflection and solitude.

1. **What do I find my mind is attracted to in times of silence and why?** This helps me to determine what I really value emotionally. For example, during a day in which I deliberately sat in my office without answering the phone or reading my email, I found that I kept wondering if I had received an email from a particular person with whom I serve on a non-profit board. Earlier in the week, I disagreed with this person in a board meeting and we had exchanged polite conflicting emails. I realized that although I had no intention of changing my position, I very much wanted this person's approval.

When I realized this, I also began to reflect on other emails and phone calls and recognized a pattern. Much of my connectedness had to do with gaining the approval of people. If asked why I was so busy in life, my unexamined answer would have addressed the specific circumstances of my life and my high energy level. Yet, my reflection revealed it is more the result of a character flaw than a life full of demanding circumstances. I imagine that my life is not that different from many others my age who are trying to be good in the name of doing good.

2. **When was the last time I felt that I was of worth to God?** A friend, who declares that while he has a type-A personality his life is like a B-movie, says he frequently feels that he only has worth to God when he is doing something for God. As a result, he fills his life with duties, diligence, and deeds hoping that God will feel obligated to give him this week's "Good Godly Citizen Award."

Yet when he examines this view, he finds it is a contradiction to his theology of grace. He uses this question when he finds himself whining over how busy and overworked he is. Realizing that he is operating on a practiced belief system that contradicts his stated value system gives him freedom to disconnect and feel grace rather than feeling guilt.

3. What is the content of my self-talk? All of us lecture ourselves every day regarding our lives. A thoughtful reflection regarding the content of these speeches may reveal that we have one lecture that we give over and over. That lecture for busy people is, "work harder and faster."

When we examine the leadership style of Jesus, we are surprised to learn that He never implores His followers to work harder. Jesus speaks more to the developing character and dependence on God rather than making sure that they have kept the Palm Pilot task entry filled.

We may find that we do not like solitude because we have to listen to "work harder and faster" one more time and so we avoid the replay button by avoiding solitude. But when our souls are healthy, then our self-talk will be healthy. The concept of self-talk is frequently addressed by self-help motivators and is often used to hype products and programs that are advertised on late night cable television. The primary problem with self-talk is that our talk is usually more about self than character. There is value in self-talk when we are not only careful to format the speech but also to evaluate what we are saying.

4. When I hear the voice of God, who does it sound like? The concept of a personal God is difficult to grasp. We believe in a God we cannot see or touch. We worship a God who does not use an audible voice (except to T.V. preachers with 800 numbers), and the primary information about God is found in book that is more than 2000 years old.

As small children, we often identify the voice of God with our authority figures. A child hears the voice of a parent saying "no" when he is tempted to act in a way that he knows is wrong. As adults we often find the voice of God still sounds like the voices we heard as children. A 40-something gentleman whose father was a product of the Great Depression remembers his father warning him regarding the danger of idleness. His father had a printed statement framed and hung in the hallway of their home, which read: "Idle hands reveal idols in the heart." Even as an adult when he paused in his daily quiet time to hear the voice of God, it sounded like his father. When he read Scripture, he continued to hear the voice of a task-driven but well-meaning father.

A friend of mine tape records his children reading Scripture and then listens to the tapes during times of reflection. During a three-month period in which he was receiving very heavy dosages of chemo-therapy, he had several friends tape several chapters of Scripture. He would listen to them while weakened from the cancer treatment. He said hearing Scripture from voices of love rather than just the voices of an authority figure was a refreshing experience. The voice of God needs to be heard in a variety of ways, and when

God always speaks to us in the same way, it may say more about the spiritual capacity to hear than it does about God's character.

5. Where did I see the work of God today in my life? If God is present in the life of those who believe in Jesus Christ, surely I should have seen some evidence in my life. The temptation here is to look for the bizarre, unusual, or miraculous. But the God of the still, small voice is also the God who moves quietly across the dimly lit areas of the stage of our life.

Recently, before I had a luncheon with a couple that needed my help, I prayed that God would give the words that might help resolve the dilemma they were facing with their adult child. I listened but never added anything of substance to any of the options they were considering. When I wrote in my journal about the experience, I cynically wrote that I was quite sure my lack of insight had been appreciated.

Yet later that day I realized that I had not caved in to my natural desire to give advice even when I do not have advice to give. For years I had prayed for the gift of silence and today I had experienced it. It was a gift from God. I had experienced the presence of God.

6. Who is intersecting my life that appears to be sent from God? Years ago, a homebound lady introduced me to the concept that angels are not always divinely created supernatural beings who make temporary appearances in your life. Angels can be other people whom God is using at specific moment. Angels can have names like Tom, Cindy, Linda, or Bob.

I once visited an elderly lady in her home who was recovering from stroke. Her illness left her with a weak body, strong mind, and slow speaking skills. While I was there, she introduced me to her nursing attendant whom she said was angel from God. She slowly explained that she had been praying for someone to stay with her so she would not have to be moved away from her home. This lady who answered the want ad section of the local paper was an outstanding caregiver. The elderly lady said, "The word *angel* simply means messenger from God." Then she asked, "Gary, who are angels God has sent to you lately?"

7. What have I learned about God today? Reflection can be narcissistic. The concept of narcissism is based on the mythological story of a young boy who observed a reflection of himself in a pool. If all I do is look and see my own strengths, weaknesses, and opportunities, I have used my day as a mirror of my life rather than a window on life. God's ultimate revelation of Himself is Jesus, the Christ. But often we assume the only place we can see Jesus is in Scripture, in church, or in acts of service. While many would prefer God would reveal the future to us, God most often is revealing His character. We are much better prepared to deal with the future when we know God's character than when we know what is going to happen next. An acquaintance of mine keeps what he calls a "God journal," in which he writes down how and what he has experienced God each day. At the end of the week as part of his Sunday evening ritual, he reexamines these experiences to make sure that what he thought he was learning about God is consistent with what is revealed in Scripture.

Reflection and solitude are not synonymous, but you will not have one without the other because they travel in tandem. Making time for reflection is part of the solitude process, but genuine solitude is more than a time management issue. Many of us will not have the opportunity for reflection until we control our time. Solitude is a character issue because it requires us to look at our inner being for worth rather than at the connectedness that has been our false source of self-worth.

But there does need to be a word of caution regarding solitude for adults. When we were in our teenage years, parents and youth workers continually spoke of the need for quiet time. Even if the quiet time was not for religious purposes, we did need to slow down and recharge our physical batteries. While that is still needed at midlife, some have used this solitude as an occasion to fume and fret. Withdrawing for spiritual nourishment for the soul and pulling back for the purpose of feeling sorry for yourself can look the same to an observer. Solitude requires diligent self-discipline in not only providing the time but making sure you really practice solitude and not holy sitting.

Several years ago two well-known aging religious leaders, who were both in their mid-80s, shared their wisdom with a room of young ministers and college and seminary professors. One of the mature leaders spoke of the necessity of pulling aside every morning for reading, study, and prayer. He told these aspiring scholars and preachers not to allow anyone to steal their morning time with administrative duties, appointments, or visiting hospitals unless it were absolutely necessary.

The other aging legend said he would like to reinforce everything the other minister said but with one caveat. He said if they were sitting in their study every day and protecting their time the way a banker guards

> *Withdrawing for spiritual nourishment for the soul and pulling back for the purpose of feeling sorry for yourself can look the same to an observer.*

his money and not growing in their understanding of God and of humanity, and brooding about how life is tough and people are mistreating them, then let yourself be interrupted, visit the hospital, and do administration. Sitting and brooding is worse than not sitting at all. In the name of solitude, we can brood over the past and breed more despair and call it reflection. Everyone does that sometimes, but there has to be the self-awareness to know when it is happening.

There is a word of hope regarding solitude. While solitude is not intended to be a time saver or a means of increasing productivity, it can do both. When we experience solitude, it often helps us hit the reset button on our life. As a result of the solitude that leads to serenity, we find that we do have a better handle on our time and our energy. Solitude can do for your life what you thought the last time management seminar would do for you. But when you practice solitude with the goal of good for goodness' sake, it is not you but God who has a handle on your life.

CHAPTER 6

The Value of Gratitude

The Rolling Stones Expressed the Feeling Right but Got the Thought Wrong with "I Can't Get No Satisfaction"

I CAN'T GET NO SATISFACTION" by the Rolling Stones may have been our generation's national anthem. Although the Rolling Stones were singing about sex, the real mistress of the baby boomers was, is, and will be money and possessions. There is no need to develop medication that helps prolong the greed drive in the senior adult years. A Viagra-like drug designed to stimulate the desire for money will never need to be marketed by those who are attempting to cash in on the aging of America. The desire for more possessions does not appear to dwindle or decline with age. Only the kind of possessions and not the amount of possession we desire that changes as we get older.

For a number of years, some economists have assumed that when the glut of babies born between 1948 and 1964 hit the magic five-zero, we would see massive downsizing in lifestyle. Some city planners and construction consultants confidently predicted that these mature adults, desiring to live frugally during their fixed income years, would sell their four- and five-bedroom houses with three-car garages and move into garden homes, condominiums, and smaller town-houses. While a few did buy smaller houses, even more purchased mountain homes, beach condos, and vacation villas and kept their large homes as well. The housing market has been dramatically impacted by the number of people who own two residences. A surprising number of baby boomers took advantage of the lower interest rates and bought or built larger homes. Even the art market is reacting to the increasing number of adults who are purchasing expensive (and sometimes tasteful) art to display in their newer or larger homes. People have more walls to display paintings so they had to purchase more art to cover the walls.

Our generation has not given up their toys. They have only replaced them with more expensive ones. Consumerism apparently has not even yet reached its peak; our thirst for more is far from satisfied by the abundance we experienced in our youth because we realize there is still so much to want.

Greed—Our Favorite Sin

While greed may be one of the seven deadly sins, our generation appears to be convinced that it should be moved from the vice side of the ledger to the virtue side. In the movie *Wall Street*, Gordon Gekko proclaimed, "Greed is good." Although these words are not a statement of revealed truth, too often they reflect our values. Not only does Scripture teach us that greed is one of the characteristics of fallen humanity, but a casual observation of the great amount of greed-induced suffering also makes us aware of the intrinsic evil of greed. While every generation has come face to face with greed, rarely has a generation of folks enjoyed, cultivated, and honored the vice as much as those born after the end of World War II and before the conclusion of the Vietnam War.

Our tendency toward greed may have been fueled by the economic knowledge that we could possess that which was never available to the masses before. Rarely in times of economic recession have the rank and file Americans been aware that increased spending could turn around the economy. Buying on credit was presented as an almost patriotic duty, as it appears that we can spend our economy out of a recession. Add this to the fact that we are the first generation to be able to spend without having to go through a demeaning loan application process that requires the borrower to sit before an employee of the bank and recite their economic history. We began to have credit cards for which we never even applied.

Because we carry our credit cards with us at all times, we also had access to the goose that laid the golden egg. In one of the great number of televised simulated trial shows where folks take small claims disputes and present their arguments to a retired photogenic judge with pithy one liners, a defendant said she was a good money manager. To prove the accuracy of her statement she proudly said that she had never been denied a credit card and had never filed for bankruptcy. Yet she did admit that she frequently purchased items with those credit cards that she could not afford.

We will not fully understand the danger of greed if we limit its definition to the desire for more money. The more accurate picture of greed is to see it as the desire for more. We have felt that we deserve more of everything, including more food, more sex, and more youth. As a result, this passion for more has made obesity a national health issue, pornography the most common addiction, and cosmetic surgery an accepted rite of passage. Almost all major cities have seen a dramatic increase in the number of rental self-storage units. While these units were originally designed for apartment dwellers, they are now being marketed to baby boomers who have 4,000 square feet in their house but still need a place to store their stuff. Their closets, attics, and garages are full.

We never get enough! Borrowing a phrase from Susan Powter, a woman of the baby boomer generation who had her moment of fame through an infomercial, we ask the question: "How do we stop the insanity?" We have learned that "just say no" did not stop the desire for drugs, and common sense and our experience teaches us that just saying no does not eliminate desire for anything.

It is not enough to curse the darkness of greed. We must cut a hole through it. And when we do, what will we find? We will find a character issue that is much larger than economics. The journey toward good character will not be moved forward until we are willing to tame the vicious beast of greed.

The Antidote

Gratitude is the antidote for greed. While different philosophers and religious traditions have frequently suggested that generosity was the antonym of greed, it is not the remedy for greed. Gratitude must precede generosity or else generosity becomes one more way of helping us get what we want. Generosity is observable and a greatly praised habit in our culture and can easily become very manipulative. The tax code has even been tilted in favor of helping us to be generous, as one motivation seminar promoted: "Learn how to make generosity profitable."

During the last decade in a major southern city, a very successful entrepreneur gave generously to a variety of not-for-profit groups and civic organizations. In response to his giving, the local municipalities and organizations named buildings, streets, and sporting facilities in honor of him and his family. When this creative financial genius was accused of being too creative and was indicted on over 50 counts of fraud by masking losses and embellishing profits and corporate net worth, community support turned against him and charitable institutions attempted to find ways to remove his name from the edifices that had been erected on their property with his money. The line to remove his name was longer than the line to return his gifts.

His generosity did not stop with the indictments; instead his giving was directed toward new organizations. Suggestions were rampant that he now only gave to organizations and ministries that reflected the profile of the jury pool. When he was acquitted in spite of almost all of his leadership team testifying against him, many in the community began to suggest his generosity was meant to benefit primarily himself. While there is no way to truly judge his motive or intent, his actions did cast a shadow over the good name of generosity.

> The virtue that eradicates greed and corrects manipulative generosity is gratitude.

Before we line up to cast stones at these folks who we assume hide a long list of sins and wrong actions behind the monument of generosity, we may need to admit that if we were God's moral prosecutors, we would have to indict ourselves. We have all learned how to use generosity to help us get more. Years ago, politicians learned that the surest way get out the vote on Election Day was to provide "walking around money" to their precinct captains in order to secure the civic duty of folks who only felt the need to become patriotic on the Tuesday following the first Monday in November in even-numbered years. Almost every major charitable board is made up of people who give or who can get others to give. If you do not help with the Red Cross, United Way, or mission support fund at church, you can be labeled non-cooperative and not a team player. Not only will your name and picture not be in the social section of the newspaper, but also your children may not be selected on the right soccer team.

A lady who is the neighborhood chairperson for a charity in our city told me that even though she really does not feel strongly about the cause for which she rings doorbells, she feels powerless to give up. She became involved in a foundation that raises money for this group when she first moved to the neighborhood. She volunteered to give a little money and some time to show that she wanted to become part of the community. Now, 10 years later, she is considered the neighborhood advocate for this particular charity. In a moment of vulnerability, she said, "It is not that I care about this charity; it is that I cannot figure out how to escape without people thinking badly of me." Would you say she is modeling goodness? When we analyze and examine her motives and actions, we may find her experiences may mirror some of the patterns that have been used to help us become generous.

The virtue that eradicates greed and corrects manipulative generosity is gratitude. One of the more common definitions of gratitude is "a feeling of thankfulness and appreciation." In the United States we even have a holiday in honor of gratitude. Yet in our generation, the day following the holiday has become more significant than the holiday itself. The Friday after Thanksgiving is now known as "Black Friday" because if sales are good on that day, it will determine if merchants are going to move out of the "red" into the "black" for the year. According to recent news media reports, some families are now in the habit of abbreviating their Thursday Thanksgiving activities so they can rise early enough to be at the malls and shopping centers for those wonderful pre-dawn Day after Thanksgiving sales. Even on the holiday to honor gratitude, it appears that greed has triumphed.

The Link Between Gratitude and Happiness

One of the most positive people I have ever known continued to work until he was in his late 80s. He was tenaciously gracious, even though he and his wife lived in a one bedroom apartment, receiving a small retirement check and supplementing his limited income with a part-time job that occasionally required his wife's assistance. While he was paid to work only 20 hours each week, it was not unusual for him to log 40 to 50 hours in any given seven-day period. He had a great sense of humor with an infectious laugh, and he obviously enjoyed life. He once told me that he had never met a happy person who was not also grateful, and he had never known an unhappy person who was grateful. Having served over 30 years of ministry in the local church and meeting a variety of folks, my experience cannot disagree with his. Gratitude and happiness appear to be linked.

Some authors suggest that depression is often linked to ingratitude, and there is some discussion as to whether ingratitude is the cause or the result of depression. While it may take years to fully sort out the relationship between the two, there is little doubt as to the fact that they are in some way intertwined. Gratitude is more than a predisposition of personality; it is a chosen attitude toward life. Several years ago, Minirth and Meier wrote a book that greatly influenced the mental health of Christians. *Happiness Is a Choice* captured this central theme by reminding the reader that happiness is more related to our will than to our circumstances. While happiness and gratitude are not identical, they are both volitional and not circumstantial issues. Gratitude is the forerunner of happiness and directly related to the quality of our emotional health. If gratitude is a chosen virtue that makes such a positive impact in our life, what are the barriers that keep us from choosing gratitude over ingratitude?

One of the most significant barriers is seeing ourselves as victims. Believing we have been cheated and mistreated in life inevitably keeps us from being grateful. Labeling our parents, spouse, employers, children, in-laws, and the government as the primary sources or causes of our failures and problems will never coexist with a thankful spirit.

Life is not fair and the privileges of life have never been nor will they ever be distributed equally; yet to bemoan that fact damages our soul and harms our character. A lady, who was in the process of losing her second child to an illness that was genetically passed to her children, told me of the anger she went through when she and her husband realized that their family was predisposed to this specific heart malady. She said, "I grew up in church, was a virgin when I was married, didn't rebel during the 1960s, exercised before it was faddish, and never smoked or consumed alcoholic beverages. And I railed at God about how unfair my life was. During the months of anger, I was impatient with my terminally ill child, of no comfort to my grieving husband, and a lonely, bitter person. But in the midst of one hellish day, I chose to see the goodness of God, not the unfairness of life as the defining truth of my existence, and I began to live again. No, my children did not survive and I did not grieve any less at their deaths. But I did live and you may not believe it, but I enjoy life. There were days the only thing for which I could be grateful was the character of God, but that was enough to help me through the awful season of the soul."

A second barrier to experiencing gratitude is thinking that our present character exempts us from the difficulties of life. Many religious types do not have difficulty acknowledging that stuff happens, but they believe, in spite of what Billy Joel's song taught, that "only the bad die young"; major tragedies will not happen to them.

There are several flaws in this type of thinking. The most prevalent flaw is that we overestimate the quality and quantity of our virtue. While good character does not protect us from hurt, most of us do not even have a realistic evaluation of our character. Many who are quick to announce they have absolute confidence in the Bible and hold to the twin evangelical shibboleths of inerrancy and infallibility find it difficult to apply the words of Matthew 19:17 to themselves. When we read, "There is none good but one, that is, God" (KJV), we assume that those words are targeted to the self-righteous people we don't like. If we think we are good, then we are not good. It is reminiscent of the line from *Catch 22* by Joseph Heller: "How can he see he's got flies in his eyes if he's got flies in his eyes?" Great question. How can you know if you have good character if your vision is always blocked by the character flaw of self-deception?

People who think they are good often are not only incapable of seeing their flaws but also have convinced themselves there is no reason to be grateful. Few people who think they are good openly admit it because that would invalidate their self-evaluation. Yet, despite our attempts to appear like we are confessing our sin, deep in our souls we hear whispers and rumors of our own goodness. The problem is we may never realize that we started the rumors.

Moral conceit is a temptation for all people, but the probability that we yield to the temptation increases after decades of being told by our parents, our teachers, Dr. Phil, and Oprah that we are special. We have to be good if the causes of bad character are poverty and lack of education. We possess more things and have more degrees than the worthy officers of the Masonic lodge. Yet these paper trophies that baby boomers were taught to cherish not only fail to provide goodness, but also can keep us from being grateful. While we would like to think that our character protects us like a crown protects royalty, our character is often more like a cross we choose to bear.

The character exemption issue is one few would openly admit but may be more common than we would like to think. As a parent of three daughters, I had great joy attending the college graduation ceremonies of all three. When our youngest completed her degree, I found that I was proud not only of her achievement, but also of her mother and father's parenting skills. I remember my wife saying to me as we sat with our two other daughters and watched the third receive her diploma, "This is so much more than we deserve." I thought this achievement was the result of two caring parents who were willing to sacrifice for their children. Then, I began to mentally list all the things we had done right as parents. I was quite proud of the fine job we had done. Yes, we were blessed, but I was convinced that the blessings were closely related to what we had done.

> When our youngest completed her degree, I found that I was proud not only of her achievement, but also of her mother and father's parenting skills.

While celebrating as a family in a local restaurant later in the day, a gentleman I know from a local civic club stopped at our table, and we told him our reason for gathering. He congratulated us and then said as he looked at our three beautiful daughters, all college graduates, "You really are blessed." While my wife's words triggered thoughts of pride, his were more like darts of humility. I knew his story. If parenting skills could be measured by a standard test he would most definitely be an award winner. Yet two of his four children had experienced great difficulty. One child had a learning disability that caused a lack of confidence. She had worked at a variety of jobs at the lowest end of the economic food chain with very little success. He and his wife had provided an excellent home life and years of private tutoring and had attempted to bolster her feeling of self worth. His first son had achieved academically and was educated at one of the nation's more prestigious schools. But the son rebelled against the parents' values while in graduate school and wanted nothing to do with his parents. This man's remark made me aware that ingratitude insidiously had slipped into my heart through the door of self-congratulation. Believing that my children's accomplishments were the result of my good character kept me from being grateful.

A third barrier to gratitude is mental laziness. When we experience good, our mental default folder is always "self" because of the universal flaw in human nature. We immediately assume that either we caused the good or deserved the good. If we expect to be a grateful person, we must deliberately engage our minds in the process.

M. Scott Peck, the psychiatrist who became to baby boomers what Dr. Spock was to their parents, often wrote of the power and danger of sloth, even suggesting that it was the original sin. Because we are physically active, materially ambitious, and willing to work the long hours those younger folks refuse to, we assume that sloth or laziness does not inhabit our lives. Yet, laziness often does slide into our pattern of thinking.

One danger of midlife is limiting our reading or thinking to subjects that reinforce what we already know or believe. Americans are very quick to ask "why" when tragedy or misfortune strikes. We rarely ask "why" when we experience unexpected good, although it is a great occasion to address the "why me" issue. When we recognize that the benefits of life that have fallen on us were not pulled by us but pushed by others, we then open the door to gratitude.

One of the most common and insidious ways we numb ourselves, limit our critical thinking, and stifle our ability to be grateful is by watching too much television. Even though we frequently chastise our children for allowing television to dominate their lives and quote the line "Television is the chewing gum of the mind," there is significant evidence that addiction to television is as predominant to middle-aged adults as to any of the younger generations. While I do not know of studies to support this observation, I find that the more people watch television the less likely they are to be grateful.

There may be several reasons television viewing inhibits gratitude. First, very little television programming promotes critical thinking and to a great extent even inhibits mental examination. Part of the reason for television's failure to provide thoughtful material can be laid at the doorstep of advertisers who are not eager to sponsor this type of programming. But there is also a problem that is involved with the very nature of the medium. When reading a book, the reader can stop at any time and reflect on an idea; however in television the show goes on, interrupted only by commercials that are crafted to grab your attention. While viewing television, if by chance an idea is introduced, the only time you can wrestle with the implications of the concept is after the end of the program. By that time your senses have been bombarded with many other thoughts and feelings.

Recently, I was discussing with a college professor friend of mine a documentary that both he and I had seen on the Discovery Channel. He casually mentioned that although the program was good, it was similar in educational value to the series of films that Bell Telephone Company had produced and were known as the Bell Telephone Science Hour. These films, hosted by Dr. Frank Baxter, were produced for schools and used from 1955 to 1975 in elementary schools throughout the nation. At the time they were described as simple, informative, and at an educational and language usage level that even children could comprehend. But now that similar programs are targeted for adult audiences, it appears that they have been "dumbed down." Because the viewer could not stop and ask questions or think through the concepts, the content of the presentation had to be very simple. The problem was not that the producers wanted to talk down to the audience; the medium of video and television are not suited for critical thinking issues. Video and television, which are not interactive, are rarely capable of leading participants through the critical thinking process.

> *While viewing a television, if by chance an idea is introduced, the only time you can wrestle with the implications of the concept is after the end of the program.*

Second, television focuses on the sensational, and as result, gives greater attention to the negative news. While it is easy to be critical of the media for being "bad news bearers," they do operate in a "bull and bear" environment that cannot ignore ratings and must keep a stream of income flowing through high ratings.

During and immediately after Hurricane Katrina, television coverage of this natural disaster was continuous. Whenever you turned on the television, you would see pictures that touched your heart and placed a cloud over your soul. The storm impacted our city by interrupting our electrical power for several days, although there was only minor damage to homes or businesses, and by sending many evacuees to our area to find temporary lodging. While we had been spared significant damage, there was almost a pall over our city.

During the first couple of days there was gratitude expressed that the full impact of the storm had missed our city, but soon the negative feelings and thoughts were expressed. We noticed a significant difference between the people who became involved in the disaster relief process and those whose involvement was primarily through watching television and sending cash to help in recovery.

Our church sent ten teams to the region, manned a local shelter, and sent trucks with bottled water, diapers, and survival supplies. The people who participated came back with a much more grateful attitude than those whose only contact with the disaster was through media. One of the more reflective ladies who served on our Operation Renew Hope teams that were sent to the heavily damaged areas commented that it was not viewing the devastation that stimulated the gratitude, but interacting with the people in that region and seeing their hope. Television viewers tend to be negative because the seeds planted in their minds are negative. You do reap what you sow.

Third, television viewing can inhibit gratitude because in the fullest sense of the word, television makes us spectators. It is similar to attending an athletic event and seeing your team being defeated and knowing there is nothing you can do about it. A couple of years ago two football fans in Alabama were watching their favorite college team lose to the in-state rival, which they believed was not only a sub-par team but an inferior one. One of the two shot and wounded the other. Fortunately, the injury was not serious. When asked by an arresting officer why he shot his friend, his reason was, "We were getting beat and I had to do something." No doubt alcohol not only contributed to the shooting but also to his response to the law enforcement officer. Television viewing can make a person feel powerless because we tend to be spectators watching our own world. Powerless people seek ways to regain power, which often leads to disaster. When we are resenting our state of powerlessness, it is impossible to be grateful.

We were the first generation to have television shape our childhood, and unfortunately, we may be the first to allow television to limit our adult character development and to also define the entire experience of midlife. While addressing the negative power of television in the context of the value of gratitude, we have to acknowledge that it impacts the other values as well. It is a significant deterrent to developing and maintaining individual relationships and to participating in group relationships or community.

Often I do pre-marital counseling with couples, and I will ask how the couple wants their marriage to be different than that of their parents. Frequently they describe parents in their 40s or 50s as strangers who come home after work, eat the meal they picked up at a drive-through window, and then watch television, often in separate rooms, with the husband going to sleep on the couch and the wife going to bed. Sometime in the night, the husband turns off the television and goes to bed. As one young bride-in-waiting said, "If all I knew about my parents was gained by what I have observed in the last five years, I would think I was probably born of a virgin."

There is nothing new under the sun except to the person who does not know history, and then everything is new.

Obviously her humor was hyperbole, but what she described apparently is more common than we would like to believe. I was surprised in this particular lady's comments because I knew her parents and would consider them active and vibrant. This couple had obviously done a good job of presenting a different image. But isn't that what television teaches us to do? Television not only presents an illusion, but by its very nature inspires us to be actresses and actors.

Mental laziness impacts gratitude in an additional way. It is very unlikely that people who refuse to learn will be grateful, because the process of learning makes us aware of the many blessings and benefits that have been given to us by previous generations. There is nothing new under the sun except to the person who does not know history, and then everything is new. In the act of learning, we have to face the issue that all we have in knowledge and information has been given to us by previous generations. A student is indebted or grateful to the teacher. At some point in midlife, we make a decision as to whether or not to continue learning. It may not be a conscious decision and it may be more of a process, but it is still a decision. There will be no goodness without gratitude, and there will be no gratitude without learning.

Will You Continue Learning?

The marketplace has been discovering that continuing education can be fertile ground for investment dollars because the growing adult market is willing to pay money to attend classes, participate in seminars, and read books. Yes, people are saluting the flag of adult education, but is learning taking place or is it an attempt to avoid the hard work of the mind and the soul? Many of the learning opportunities being offered are marketed as shortcuts to the hard and disciplined task of learning.

Learning is definitely more than taking a class on photography or finding new ways to tax shelter your money so you will be able to give your grandchildren more toys at Christmas instead of investing with more tax dollars in their education. An acquaintance who occasionally teaches night classes in the adult education department of a local junior college told me when he first began teaching adults he was optimistic and excited about how the trend of adults going back to class could make a major impact on society. But now that he has five years of experience in night classes, he has developed a low grade level of cynicism and pessimism. He was surprised at how many of the adult students were only interested in refresher classes that helped them remember what they had learned the first time they were in school. Also at his college, many adults registered for computer classes and attended a few sessions but never completed the course. Once they learned how to be proficient enough to make purchases on the Internet, use email, and open the pictures their college kids sent them, they ceased attending. Still others only take classes that they think will answer specific questions. This appears to be the case at some of the seminary and divinity schools that offer classes for the laity at nights or on Saturdays. Classes that promise to help understand *The Da Vinci Code* or the Book of Revelation often are filled in the opening sessions, but when these adults realize they will have to read books and grapple with philosophical questions, they stay home and watch HGTV.

While some midlifers avoid learning like it was cholesterol, others are recognizing that this stage of life is the first time they have the experience and confidence to face very difficult and complex issues. A lady who has been a member of an evangelical church all her life and passed the litmus test of her particular denomination began a thorough study of Christian philosophy and theology by enrolling in night classes and taking some online courses. She read books recommended by her pastor, as well as books suggested by a Catholic priest, and even some articles that an agnostic work acquaintance gave her. She gleaned the daily newspapers to find announcements of guest lecturers coming to different churches and attended as many as she could. Some thought she was in a midlife crisis, but her explanation was, "I am in midlife confidence. For the first time in my life I feel capable of examining opposing views without being threatened. I am not fearful of losing my faith, but I was concerned that I may have short-changed my faith by never dealing with hard questions and only accepting the answers of others who had studied more difficult issues." Her study made her more appreciative of her heritage of faith, as well as of those who differed with her on religious and philosophical matters.

> *Some thought she was in a midlife crisis, but her explanation was, "I am in midlife confidence."*

Lifelong learning builds gratitude because it is more than just taking courses and getting certification. This may be what distinguishes it from the learning experiences of youth and college years. We attended classes in order to get grades for the purpose of receiving diplomas that would help us secure jobs. It is an attitude that causes us to interact with people on different levels. Lincoln is a 48-year-old certified public accountant who changed employers in the last three years. He was required by the new employer to take some additional professional classes and to become certified in a specific area. He reluctantly did so, but after completing it he also has done two other professional certifications. His friends have questioned whether these last two would provide any career or financial benefit. Lincoln quickly tells his friends that he does not attend classes for money, career status, or to have more initials after his name. He attends because he is learning much about life by interacting with adults who have had different life experiences than he has had. I have observed that he is a much more patient man who has become a better listener and appears to have lost some of the angry edge that limited him. While he might not use the word to describe himself, I see him as a grateful person.

Gratitude Will Change Your Life

While the concept of gratitude and learning may not be related in professional education circles, most teachers, regardless of whether they teach the young or the old, will quickly acknowledge that their best learners are grateful. Gratitude is both a cause and result of learning, and it can become a victorious cycle. The old eastern proverb that says, "When the student is ready to learn the teacher will appear," is a way of acknowledging that our attitude governs the amount of learning we experience.

Several families have relocated from the Gulf Coast to the city where I live as a result of the devastation of Hurricanes Dennis and Katrina in the late summer and fall of 2005. The local school systems had to adapt quickly and provide classrooms and help teachers adjust to having many temporary students. Many of the students have had to stay much longer in their new schools than they originally anticipated and are often living with friends or extended family. One child was able to return to his home school after one semester. He carried with him copies of his grades from his old school and his principle was surprised to learn that this fourth grade boy had made all A's and B's at the school in our area. The principal assumed the teachers had been more generous in grading out of sympathy. Although he did not know the student's teacher, he did know the excellent reputation of the school system and the student's accomplishments were even more surprising. Later he would learn the events of the hurricane had caused a major shift in the family's attitude. Being so overwhelmed by the outpouring of love by friends, family, and the community of which they were temporary residents, they, in turn, had become grateful. Seeing what others had done for them created a healthy sense of duty and obligation. Since others had given so much, he and his family felt they must do their best. Gratitude enlarged the child's learning capacity, and the more he learned the greater his capacity for gratitude expanded.

Gratitude is not only a healthy step toward expanding the mind, but it is a necessary step in building character!

CHAPTER 7

The Value
of Forgiveness

Meat Loaf Got It Right When He Sang
"Objects in the Rear View Mirror
May Appear Closer Than They Are"

A PSYCHIATRIST FRIEND AND I occasionally go to lunch together. He tells me our meetings are for the purpose of keeping me sane, and I respond that the real purpose is to keep him holy. Our spouses say if our efforts are to be measured by our results, then both of us have failed. More than once he has said that the issue most of his clients must grapple with at some time in their therapy is forgiveness. While some need desperately to forgive people who have either wounded them or who they perceive has wounded them, others need to be forgiven for hurting someone else. Some clients need to experience divine forgiveness and some need to forgive themselves.

As I think of the people who have entered my office for spiritual and pastoral help over the years, most of them needed to engage in either the work of receiving or giving grace. I am not a counselor by training or by gift, but many people have come to see a pastor with a variety of complaints, burdens, and frustrations. As I mentally download my calendar of appointments, almost all of them are searching for someone to tell them they are forgiven or give them guidance on how to forgive others. As I think about my own issues with forgiveness past and present, the quality of my life is better when I forgive and worse when I am unforgiving.

On a recent holiday, I replayed a conversation with a man over and over again in my mind, missing much of the joy of the day. Although we would never agree on the issue that started the conversation, I realized that my choice of words revealed more about past hurts than the merits of the argument. I thought how I might have begun the conversation differently, because my opening words had been spoken in anger. This damaged conversation was the result of some hurt I had experienced in a previous conversation. I realized that I had tried to get even rather than get over it. The person who is forgiven and forgiving will conduct life much differently than the one who allows unresolved guilt to influence attitude and behavior. If forgiveness ran like water through our minds, in our hearts, and off our lips, it would change our family gatherings, staff meetings, and communities.

Forgiveness for Wounds Received

Forgiveness is not a virtue that is just appropriate for one age group, but the need for it may be greater at midlife. By the time we are 40 years of age, most adults have more hurts than a hypochondriac with non-deductible health insurance. Over the years, we have accumulated hurt, rejection, and disappointment, and unfortunately the mind is like Velcro when we have been wounded. We rarely forget past hurts.

Over the years, we have accumulated hurt, rejection, and disappointment, and unfortunately the mind is like Velcro when we have been wounded.

We are wise and experienced enough to know where our parents failed and how their imperfect parenting damaged our life. Jesus had no children, so none of us can say our parents were perfect. Although we admit they may have, for the most part, been good parents, we do know they still made mistakes that impacted us. Words and actions by colleagues have left their mark because we have either been stepped on or we have stepped on someone in order to climb the career ladder.

Then, if we are parents, we learn the reality that children are not only a blessing from God, but they can also be nature's way of punishing us for every bad thing we said and thought about our parents. Sometime around the age of 40 if not earlier we have given up the illusion that on judgment day God will give us the "perfect parenting award" in front of all our peers who were just average parents. Our children have never risen up and called us blessed unless they wanted something, but they have risen up many times to blast us rather than bless us.

As parents we carry guilt and regret for our mistakes, impatience, and frustrations with our children. Years ago, a homiletic instructor in seminary told his students that if their primary purpose in preaching was to have people make public decisions, then they should preach on motherhood every Sunday and invite mothers to come and confess their guilt and failures. The wise professor said you would have the altars full every Sunday. But the experienced preaching professor continued by reminding us that the goal of preaching was changed lives, and that could only be done by preaching grace.

Forgiveness for Wounds Inflicted

As you mature, you are not only aware of the hurts you have received, but you become more aware of the wounds you have inflicted upon others. The wisdom that you have accumulated has also made you aware that some of the hurt you inflicted on others was not as accidental as the younger and immature mode you had once claimed. The words and deeds through which you harmed people may not have been the result of carefully thought-out strategies designed to hurt people, but maturity makes you aware that some things you have done that caused pain were done with a poison purpose buried in your mind.

Years ago I hurt a man's feelings by telling him something that was painfully true but unnecessary on a day when he was celebrating a great victory. My words took the wind out of his sails and while my remarks certainly did not cause it to rain on his parade, it did definitely create a small dark cloud. I later apologized for my poor timing, but only recently did I realize it was not as much a slip of the tongue as an exposure of the ego. While I was friends with this individual, I also was competitive with him. I doubt that I would have spoken these words to another individual, but I now realize that my words flowed from my insecure competitive nature rather than because I was just careless. My self-worth at that particular stage of life was primarily measured through comparing myself to others. I am quite certain I am not the only person who has used words as weapons when they had more ambition than goodness.

During the early stages of adulthood, we may not recognize the extent of the hurt and sorrow we have caused others. Our lack of experience in life and our self absorption in career and family contribute to this lack of sensitivity regarding others. But when we have given up on being the president of the world and have realized that our children and spouse no longer worship us, we start to recognize the real extent of the sinful nature that is within us.

Several years ago the *New York Times* printed an obituary that included one of the last statements of the deceased. This man, who had achieved some notoriety in his lifetime, was quoted as saying just a few days before he died that he now realized that for most of his life he had been "a real jerk." It would have been interesting to hear the reactions to that statement by the man's family, friends, and professional colleagues when they read his obituary. No doubt they would agree that he had spoken the truth because they carried the scars of having been wounded by this "real jerk." Midlife provides an opportunity to acknowledge, name, and confront the weapons we have used to inflict hurt on others.

Often the virtues of relationships and community are marred or minimized by the way we have treated others. We may have to walk through the valley of confession before we experience the fresh and cleansing water of forgiveness flowing over our troubled soul. What we may have once labeled as personality conflicts or irreconcilable differences may have had little to do with personality or differences and more to do with our indifference to grace and forgiveness. A self-confessed loner once told me that he thought his propensity to being aloof was not about being an introvert but a technique he had learned to avoid having to admit that he was wrong. It was just easier to avoid relationships than to have to deal with the stuff of hurt and broken relationships. He did not like to admit that he was wrong or to forgive those who had wronged him.

Others go into midlife with years of accumulated anger over past hurts and unaware of how the unresolved anger has impacted their lives and damaged their families. Daily they relive the harsh words, the unfair accusations, and the feelings of abandonment. Yet they very rarely tell others why they are so angry. Medication and therapy have helped these unhappy folks to survive and to see another day, but deep within them there is a desire to thrive and live another way. The only balm that can heal the deeply troubled soul is forgiveness.

Forgiveness Brings Healing—for You

Eric worked hard, played little, and was serious about the tasks assigned him. But he was not accomplished at playing office politics and unknowingly participated in some activities that caused him to appear to be disloyal to the leadership team. At age 36, he was terminated with very little severance pay, while the real disloyal villains covered their actions and allowed Eric to be "thrown under the bus." Not only did Eric and his family suffer financially, he was also embarrassed at being fired and very angry at himself for being so naïve about people.

This company was known for its commitment to conservative family values and that encouraged their employees to attend office prayer meetings. Eric had bought the company line and both he and his wife assumed they would be protected from the evil corporate world. This company annually made a contribution to Focus on the Family and was the grand marshal in the family values parade. Eric did find another job, but it took five years before his annual salary equaled what he had received the year he was terminated.

During those five years, bitterness became the mistress of Eric's soul, and Eric's wife not only was angry at what the company had done to him, but failed to understand why Eric could not get over it. Meaningful communication decreased between him and his wife as they primarily exchanged in sharing information instead of feelings. Just as the parents lived emotionally in separate worlds, so did their children. Their house was more like a residence for four people rather than a family home. There was no war of words between them and no threat of abuse; silence was their weapon of choice in their cold war.

> *Good character and bitterness will not live in the same heart, and the resolution to bitterness always involves forgiveness.*

Realizing that there was little joy in their marriage, they had to make a decision regarding their future. They could go the divorce route and write the official obituary for their marriage or go for counseling. They chose counseling not as a means of restoring romance, but because both Eric and his wife realized that a divorce could place his present job and salary in jeopardy, and they would have to drop down a level in lifestyle. Money, more than love, called them to marriage counseling.

They did not expect the counseling to bring much joy to their lives and just hoped it might lessen the pain and protect their toys. After several sessions of hearing their stories, the trained therapist told them that the only time either of them spoke with real passion in their voice was when they were describing the events and circumstances around his firing. Eric thought he had known everything that happened to them but was surprised to hear his wife say that even the other corporate wives did not acknowledge her existence after he was let go. Eric cried for her for the first time. When Eric's wife told how devastating it was to see him curled up in the fetal position in the bed and how she had prayed that he would not commit suicide, it was evident that she still had feelings for him. It was evident that neither Eric nor his wife had forgiven anyone, including each other, related to the firing. They could not replace that chapter in their lives, but they could start to heal by forgiving each other and those who initiated the problem. Forgiveness would precede improvement in their marriage.

Good character and bitterness will not live in the same heart, and the resolution to bitterness always involves forgiveness. Forgiveness may be the most difficult virtue to consistently activate in our life. Revenge, bitterness, and self-pity are so woven into the fabric of fallen human nature that we may think that they are right responses. The litigation society that has emerged during our lifetime makes no allowance for forgiveness. We no longer follow the Biblical command that, "Vengeance is mine...saith the Lord" (Romans 12:19 KJV), and we have replaced it with "Vengeance is mine saith the man with the most expensive attorney."

Even in Christian circles, people are surprised when an offended party does not go to court. A small non-profit organization in the southwest was delighted when their lawyer informed the board that a potential lawsuit against a vendor might net them three times their annual budget. This was in spite of the fact that the vendor had already offered to settle for actual losses. A board member offered to personally give money to hire a "heavyweight" plaintiff law firm to argue their side of the case. His generosity would allow the charity's public relations committee to announce to the donating public that none of their contributions were being used in the lawsuit. They did not want to look like the revengeful people they actually were. Although wiser heads did prevail and the board chose not to litigate, several board members did resign believing that the failure to go to court was an act of fiduciary irresponsibility. It is difficult for midlife baby boomers to be forgiving, for we are swimming against the current of culture.

Resentment Replay

Few of our generation would disagree that forgiveness is a virtue, but many would like to define or describe forgiveness to fit their comfort level. The verb *forgive* in English refers to the giving up of resentment or of a claim. While the religious meaning of forgiveness goes somewhat further, it does not negate this meaning. This is a great place to start understanding the nature of forgiveness. People who are bitter and angry replay the story of their hurts over and over in their mind. Each time they do, they feel the same emotions they did when the hurt occurred. This re-sensing becomes resentment, which is the foundation of bitterness.

Our generation has the technology to allow us to see and to hear the events of the past over and over again. Few if any of the events from our parents' lives were ever placed on film. We were the first generation to be able to have home movies. Recently, I attended the 50th birthday celebration of a lady, during which they showed home movies of her childhood. The movies were not great quality, but when her sister, who is eight years younger, has her 50th, there will be more and better pictures. I later learned that this birthday girl did not like one particular home movie that was shown because it brought up some painful memories from her childhood. Through audio tapes and videos we not only have memories flowing across of the screen of our mind, we can make yesterday appear on the big screens in our houses. One of the side effects is that the old feelings begin to emerge within us. It is difficult to forgive when we choose to re-experience our hurts over and over again.

At midlife we have a choice to make about our past hurts. We can bury them deep into our memory hard drive by ignoring them, we can choose to even the score with the people who hurt us, or we can choose to forgive. Sounds like an easy choice. But the forgiveness road is not only less traveled, it can also be the most bumpy and uncomfortable, especially for the first few miles of the journey.

Jesus promised His followers that their walk with Him would not be easy. He continually warned them of persecution, crosses to bear, and rejection—even by family. Rarely do we think of the life of forgiveness in terms of rejection and pain. But when we choose to be forgiving, we may experience more pain than ever. Forgiving people are often rejected and are perceived to be simple and naïve. Yet, without forgiveness there is no character. Without forgiveness, there can be no relationship with Christ. The beginning point for a forgiving way of life is a choice.

Jesus Requires It

While the pain that results from being unforgiving is often the first wake-up call during our nightmare of bitterness, it usually is not the intensity of the present pain or the allure of the peace we will gain that pulls us in the forgiveness lane of the character highway. For most, the awareness of the need to make a choice to forgive comes from realizing that forgiveness is a requirement of the Christian faith. A 43-year-old father of three was informed by his physician that he was going to have to change where he worked. Needing only six more years until he could qualify for retirement, he asked his physician, "Do I really have to?" The physician carefully explained that he had a very rare allergic reaction to a chemical that was needed in much of the work he did in a research laboratory. The physician concluded, "You only need to change if you want to live, but if that is not real important to you, stay where you are, and you will never retire, but you will expire." The employee said, "Well, since you explained that way, I think I will choose to change occupations."

Jesus explained that if you want life with the Father through Jesus the Son, then you have to forgive. Forgiveness is not an option for the super holy, but a commanded virtue for all who claim to use the Christian label. While Jesus did not address every issue of life in language of black and white, He did speak directly to the issue of forgiveness frequently.

Jesus made certain His followers saw forgiveness as a required commandment and not just another opportunity to improve their emotional health. In the Sermon on the Mount, Jesus addressed forgiveness, and in the Lord's Prayer He taught us to pray for forgiveness as we forgive each other. Then, in order to remove all doubt and to ensure they would not think they could find some wiggle room in His teachings regarding the relationship between God's forgiveness of us and our forgiveness of others, Jesus says in Matthew 6:14–15: "For if you forgive men when they sin against you, your heavenly Father will also forgive you. But if you do not forgive men their sins, your Father will not forgive your sins." Jesus made sure that His followers knew He was not expecting them to do the occasional good deed of forgiveness when in Luke 17:3–4 He says, "So watch yourselves. If your brother sins, rebuke him, and if he repents, forgive him. If he sins against you seven times in a day, and seven times comes back to you and says, 'I repent,' forgive him."

> *Jesus made certain His followers saw forgiveness as a required commandment and not just another opportunity to improve their emotional health.*

Not only is Jesus the Master Teacher on the subject of forgiveness, He modeled it perfectly on the cross when He prayed for those who executed Him: "Father, forgive them, for they do not know what they are doing" (Luke 23:34). Meeting with the disciples after the resurrection, Jesus did not do a post-Good Friday grading of the performance of His support team. We all know that Judas would have received an "F" and none of the other eleven would have received a passing grade. None of them defended Him, and apparently they left Calvary during His execution more quickly than a Donald Trump-fired apprentice exits the stage.

But even greater than the accounts describing Jesus forgiving specific individuals is the redemptive meaning of the cross. In the Book of Romans, the apostle Paul unpacks the meaning of the cross in terms of forgiveness and reconciliation. Forgiveness is more than a kind act Jesus did occasionally to show that He was a good man. Forgiveness is intertwined so tightly with the message and mission of the Messiah that you cannot extract it from the Gospels without destroying who Jesus was and why He came.

Baby boomers, who grew up in a world that in their lifetime tilted away from absolutes to relativism, have difficulty hearing and accepting any absolute requirement. Few in our generation forget the signs the protesters carried outside of the Democratic National Convention in 1968 and on the opening night of the Republican National Convention in 1972: "No one has the right to take away my rights." Yet forgiveness is a command of Jesus and involves giving up the right most of us cherish, the right to be bitter. Forgiveness is more a faith matter than an emotional health and comfort issue. Make no mistake—ultimately, forgiveness removes a great amount of pain and makes us emotionally healthier. But it is not primarily about us feeling better but about us being Christian. We arrive at the decision point as a result of hearing the straightforward commands of our Lord. In some African languages, the word for *crisis* is very similar to a fork in the road. We decide to either forgive people or not to forgive people.

Once we make the decision to be forgiving, this does not mean we are forgiving people. There are many steps, some of which are recurring in the process. While the sequence of these next steps will vary from person to person, they are all necessary at some time in everyone's process.

Letting Go

Forgiveness requires the letting go of something that is or has been useful to us. If forgiveness did not require us to give up something that we perceive to be of value, we would forgive automatically and would not need the commands of Jesus to make it happen. Forgiveness would flow from us as easily as water flows downhill. Extending grace to those who have hurt or wounded us is moving against the pull of gravity. Revenge is the natural response.

For some of us, we are letting go of a coping mechanism. Bitterness is often a method of coping with the memory of past pain. To be able to be angry at someone helps us find meaning, albeit the wrong meaning, in our past. Deep in our soul is the desire to find purpose in all of life's experiences. If we see none, we then recast the battle between good and evil, and of course our side is the good side.

> *Deep in our soul is the desire to find purpose in all of life's experiences.*

Jim married his college sweetheart. They met on move-in day of their freshman year on a large state university campus. Both of them were overwhelmed with university life, but also exited about the new future they were inventing. By the end of their freshman year, they were serious, and it appeared to them that God had brought them together. Out of the 10,000 young people who entered in the largest freshman class in the university's history, they had met. What were the chances two people who had so much in common would meet on the first day?

They both had "Reagan for President" bumper stickers on their cars, they were conservative before conservatism was cool, they were planning on majoring in business, and they both liked *Star Wars V: The Empire Strikes Back.* No girl Jim had ever met liked that movie as much as he did. If this wasn't "a God thing" then "God didn't make little green apples, and it don't rain in Indianapolis in the summer time."

They were married at the end of their senior year and by the age of 30 they had two kids, a van, and a home computer. Life was good, but boring. The marriage hit the wall when they turned 38—about the time he began losing hair and she started gaining weight. First, words were the weapons between them. Then it was a new young, thin work colleague that made him think he was young and his wife was old. Although nothing physical happened between Jim and the woman in the next cubicle, there was an unhealthy emotional attachment. His wife's parents got involved and encouraged her to leave him. An angry divorce followed, including a nasty and expensive child custody fight.

Jim told everyone who would listen that, given time and professional help, he and his wife could have worked out their marriage difficulties had it not been for her parents' involvement. Looking back on earlier days in the marriage, he could now see how her parents had contributed to several of their problems.

Nearing 50, Jim married again hoping the feelings of Camelot would return. Soon his new wife told him that he obviously had some unresolved anger issues. His therapist told him that his bitterness at his ex-in-laws was destroying his new marriage. He did not want to give up those feelings because if he did, he would have to go back and reinterpret what happened in his first marriage. By staying angry at them and never forgiving them, he did not have to face his own responsibility.

For years, he ignored the fact that the reason he married the first time was because he was emotionally lazy. She had just dropped into his life, and while he first said it was God, later in his anti-religious stage, he called it fate. The emotional bonding with the young, thinner lady in the next cubicle took less work than attempting to re-bond with his wife. And now, facing the need to forgive his ex-in-laws, he again chose the easier road. The emotional affair had more to do with sloth than passion. Again he went where he found the least resistance. Staying unforgiving was much easier than facing the truth about himself. It was easier and more comfortable to see himself as the victim than to face the fact he was an emotionally lazy person.

Jim's story may be more intense than others, but it is surprising how many people follow the same path. They choose the endless pain of bitterness over the redemptive pain of forgiveness. They would rather stay angry at others rather than admit that they may have contributed to some extent to their own situations. To be forgiven and to forgive are both means of emotional healing, but some prefer sickness over health because it is less painful.

Do You Want to Be Healed?

Jesus once encountered a man who was unable to walk. Jesus asked him what appeared to be an almost ridiculous question. The man, who had been an invalid for 38 years, was sitting by a pool that was thought to have miraculous healing power. With both the miracle pool and now the "miracle man" close at hand, the man was asked by Jesus, "Do you want to be whole?" Of course the man wanted to be healed; why else would he be waiting at the pool? Didn't Jesus get it?

As always, Jesus addressed real issue. For 38 years this man had no social responsibilities. He did not have to work, provide his own food, pay taxes, go to weddings, and probably was exempt from offering sacrifices at the Temple. Though it was certainly a very difficult kind of life, he would have to give up the role of being a "kept man" if he were suddenly healed and able to walk. He would be expected to be a contributing member to the community rather than just a consumer of the generosity of others. Jesus did "get it" and addressed the heart of the issue: did the man want to give up his 38 years of coping skills in return for the responsibility of being well?

When you forgive another person, you not only set both the other individual and yourself free, but you also accept the burden of being responsible for your own spiritual and emotional health. For this reason, many adults choose not to forgive because by midlife they have learned to live in ways that compensate for the unhappiness they now have. These emotional crutches are often the myths we live by. By midlife, the lies we tell ourselves have been repeated so many times that we not only believe them, but we defend them and think they have left stains on the fabric of our souls that cannot be removed.

When attempting to install the forgiveness virtue into the hard drive of your character, it may be necessary to examine what you will lose or no longer have access to if you forgive. An acquaintance of mine who has had to experience some great pain in both forgiving and in being forgiven has a routine he goes through so he will not take forgiveness lightly. He asks himself the following three questions when he forgives someone of something he feels is significant:

1. Why is this forgiveness so difficult for me? This question deals with what he has to give up in order to forgive.

2. Am I really forgiving or am I attempting to manipulate a situation or perhaps seeking the approval of someone?

3. Why do I feel the need to forgive at this specific time? This causes him to look at forgiveness in view of the larger issues in his life. Sometimes we forgive to get it over with rather than to be godly. While this is definitely better than being unforgiving, it certainly will not qualify for the Character Hall of Fame.

This routine or discipline may be too mechanical for some, but it does require you to examine the motivations for your attempts to extend grace.

Another step in developing a lifestyle of forgiveness is to look at how being a forgiving person changes the way we relate to people. We know how withholding forgiveness can motivate. The old wisdom says, "When pushed into a corner by a good person, first lie your way out, as good people will believe anything. Second, if deception fails, then try to bribe your way out, as good people usually are poor and need money. If all else fails, make them feel guilty, as good people always think they are responsible for bad things." To be an authentically forgiving person, we can no longer be habitually motivated by guilt. Most of us have honed the art of motivation by guilt until it is sharper than a razor's edge. We have learned it from our parents, and we pass it to our children. Midlife is when we often take motivation by guilt to an even higher level.

I know more than one boomer whose parents have a crisis every time their adult children are going on vacation or participating in some pleasurable experience. One lady's mother has gone to the emergency room the last five times when her daughter has been out of town. Although she would never ask her daughter to interrupt her vacation, she does have the nurse tell her daughter to "Use your own judgment about coming home. Don't do it for me, but if it will make you and your husband feel better, I will understand." She is good at this! But so are most of us. One of my adult daughters informed me that the questions I ask often induce guilt. I responded, "Is that because you are guilty?" She replied, "As I said, your questions induce guilt."

In a visit with a group of leaders who all work in the non-profit community, we were discussing how we generally do not do very well during the holidays. Most present and involved in the discussion were self-confessed workaholics and found that less actual work is done during the holiday season because people arrive late, leave early, visit with each other during the day, and use their accumulated personal days and vacation time. As a result, we are miserable seeing so much non-productivity. We make sure the folks in our offices know that we are at work early and stay late and often are the last to leave on Christmas Eve.

One of the participants said that a senior employee told him his attempts to "guilt" people into working harder during the Christmas season was actually creating a bad work environment for January. Instead of returning refreshed from a relaxed December, the employees were returning resentful that they work for a Grinch who tried to steal their Christmas.

Forgiving people can without question hold people accountable, but motivating them to forgive primarily by guilt is inconsistent with a life of grace. While every generation has struggled with this, the first generation to grow up with television cut their emotional teeth on motivation by guilt. Many of the well-intentioned attempts by the television networks to increase our sensitivity to the racial divisions in the nation appealed to guilt and sympathy rather that to authentic goodness. As one African-American leader in our city told me, many of the news programs of the 1960s and 1970s, while showing the unfortunate plight of minorities and the poor, also implied that if we just admitted our guilt we would experience racial healing. The articulate lady, who was present during the civil rights movement marches, said "Americans are good at confessing guilt, but too often they think the mission is then accomplished." Her insight extends far beyond civil rights as we have learned that motivating by guilt produces feelings but not changes.

Forgiving Ourselves

At some point in the search for the virtue of forgiveness, we have to face the issue of forgiving ourselves.

While there has always been a need to forgive one's self, it has been addressed frequently and forcefully in our generation. One of the consistent themes of preaching in the church has been forgiveness, yet a non-scientific survey of the history of homiletics reveals that forgiveness of self was rarely addressed in preaching until the late 1950s. Forgiveness was something you accepted from God and granted to others. It was not a state of grace you bestowed upon yourself. Speaking of forgiving yourself was often seen as a way to justify your own feelings and avoid facing failures. Just as forgiving others is painful, self-forgiveness is also. We have to admit our own irresponsiblities and failures and see that these two are not the same.

The summer following my seventh grade, a baseball coach helped me to understand the difference between failing and being irresponsible. In a key game for our team, I struck out with the bases loaded in the third inning. On my next at bat, attempting to atone for earlier, I deliberately ignored a bunt sign and swung and hit a double. After the game, I apologized to the coach for striking out and was quite proud of the double that knocked in the tying run. The coach told me I did not need to apologize for striking out, as that was simply a failure to perform, but ignoring a bunt signal from the third base coach was an irresponsible action.

Getting over our failure to perform is a completely different concern. Moral responsibility is a spiritual issue. Forgiveness for the believer in Jesus Christ requires the awareness and acknowledgement that we have disobeyed God and not just that we have failed to perform at the level of our expectations. Meaningful self-forgiveness is based on the knowledge that God has forgiven us. Without the awareness and the assurance of God's forgiveness, any attempt to forgive ourselves is mere hype.

Forgiveness is rooted in our understanding of the Christian faith and in a relationship with God through Jesus Christ. Knowing that we are forgiven of our sin frees us from the burden of guilt and empowers us to forgive others. When you accept the reality that God has completely forgiven you of your sins, it eliminates the need to remind others of theirs.

> *The coach told me I did not need to apologize for striking out, as that was simply a failure to perform, but ignoring a bunt signal from the third base coach was an irresponsible action.*

A friend who is a recovering alcoholic carried rage for years over the murder of a relative and deep-seated anger toward the judicial system, which appeared to be more committed to protecting the convicted murderer than in seeing justice done. But when he fully realized that God had forgiven him for the way he had abused his body through alcohol, he then was free to forgive people in the legal system who had made mistakes in the investigation and trial. He no longer was consumed by anger and could forgive a judge for mistakes in the criminal proceedings. A quarter of a century after his relative was murdered, he wrote a letter of forgiveness to the man on death row who had taken his relative's life. He said that forgiving the convicted felon never crossed his mind until he had experienced forgiveness.

While we may have not have committed a felony, by midlife all of us know that we have made choices that have damaged and hurt others. We can punish ourselves for our mistakes and punish others for what they have done, or we can accept God's invitation to experience forgiveness and His commandment to express forgiveness.

CHAPTER 8

The Value of Humility

If the Weekly Reader Was Truthful,
Why Should We Be Humble?

I
T IS HARD TO BE HUMBLE when you are a baby
boomer. From the day we entered school, we
have been told we were special. Because there
were so many of us, they built new schools in which
to educate us. As a result, we had nicer education
facilities than the previous generation. The education
philosophy evolved while we were students to the
point that often the self-esteem of the student was as
important as the content of the class. Our teachers regularly told us to cheer up because we possessed more
potential than any other generation. They had told our
parents' generation to buckle down because they
needed to realize that they had to show concern for
everyone else, not just themselves.

Our schools provided us with the *Weekly Reader,*
which was a children's version of the *USA Today* that
would emerge for us as adults 25 years later. This
cheery little newspaper gave us a thumbnail sketch of
news events and frequently reminded us that we were
privileged to be living in the scientific revolution. We

also read that we were going to be the best-educated, healthiest, most progressive generation ever. Teachers told us that people would walk on the moon in our lifetime. We saw it become a reality even before the oldest of us graduated from college or the majority of us completed high school. We were the first generation whose nickname, "baby boomers," became a part of the everyday vocabulary.

The building epidemic followed us to college as the institutions of higher learning had to expand to take on the hoard of folks entering their doors believing that college was no longer a privilege but an inalienable right. Housing increased dramatically when we started to marry, and now the faster new housing markets are empty-nester subdivisions consisting of garden homes and townhouses.

We are still special in that both the right and left wings on the political spectrum now proclaim they are going to repair Social Security so it will have money for us. We are not surprised at the politicians catering to us; in fact, we expect it because every institution has had to adjust to us.

Humility appears to be a virtue best acquired and worn by the weak, small, and ordinary, and we are not weak, small, or ordinary. We are the baby boomers!

Yet those who travel the path toward goodness must pass through the land of humility, or they will never reach their destination. Being good for goodness' sake requires the virtue of humility. There cannot be goodness without humility. While it is wrong to assume that humility is the sum total of goodness, it is most definitely an essential component.

Although most midlifers would salute the flag of humility, it is not our signature characteristic. Historically, humility has been considered one of the traditional seven capital virtues, and on more than one occasion it has been called the heart of virtue. An early church father, John Chrysostom, suggested that humility was the greatest of all virtues. The antonym of humility is pride, which is one of the most condemned vices in all of Scripture. While few would argue its place on the throne of goodness, it does not come easy for many of our generation.

Being Humble or Being Humbled

Some have wrongly assumed that aging in and of itself creates humility. While aging may improve wine and mellow the libido, it certainly does not nullify pride. The aging process does humble, and in some circumstances, humiliate us, but being *humbled* and being *humble* are not the same thing. As one 41-year-old lady said, "Getting a hysterectomy, becoming concerned about the younger women with whom my husband works, and overhearing my son say 'No woman over 40 can ever be considered sexy' all occurred in the same month. I realized I had become my mother. Now that is humbling."

Authentic humility is more than realizing that Father Time and Mother Nature have become a tag team for the purpose of wrestling youth away from us. While this lady may have been humbled, her experience was considerably different than the humility we were able to see in Mother Teresa. Humility can result from being humbled, but not all people who have been humbled have humility. Being humbled can result in bitterness, victimization, revenge, and despair.

Allowing God to guide and direct you may not eliminate all of the humbling experiences of aging, but it does create the possibility that the aging process will become something beautiful and meaningful.

Allowing God to guide and direct you may not eliminate all of the humbling experiences of aging, but it does create the possibility that the aging process will become something beautiful and meaningful and, in that process, we will develop the virtue of humility. The pathway to humility often involves some involuntary experiences that hurt us or wound us. Then the pain that results from these hurts forces us to realize our limitations. It is possible to confuse that process with humility. Benjamin Franklin declared humility as one of the significant virtues but never appeared to make it a part of his character. His autobiography frequently points out the suffering in his life. He carried his suffering more like a crown than a cross. His humility was merely a fake walking cane that allowed people to feel sorrow for him as he aged.

Authentic humility is also more than a reaction to aging. It is a deliberate act of the will. The first step on the journey is the recognition of our own limitations.

Some adults, especially baby boomers who have been told from birth that they were unlimited, live in extended adolescence for an extra 20 years. In fact, some believe this is the root of the fascination with cosmetic surgery—the hope that if we look young, we will feel young and invulnerable. Automobile insurance companies produce commercials and mail pamphlets reminding parents that teenagers feel invincible and think they can handle a car at any speed. When you are 18 years of age, you can eat what you want and not gain weight, forgo a night's sleep and still show up without slowing up, and dance all night without dragging all day.

But about midlife, you begin to realize that regardless of the many vitamins you consume and even though you do aerobics every day, you cannot keep up with the younger Joneses. Many midlifers make appointments with their physicians to see what is wrong with them, only to find that they are in appropriate health for their age. A physician friend says he finds that many adults change physicians during their 40s because they are searching for that physician who will tell them they are unlimited, without physical boundaries. In truth, humility is first and foremost a spiritual issue that involves the Great Physician rather than the right family physician.

The Desire to Be God

The spiritual path to humility involves much more than recognizing that we are limited; it is the internal recognition and the external acknowledgement that we are not God. Adam and Eve may be the prototype of the baby boomer. There had never been anyone like Adam and Eve, and when they experienced something, they thought no one else had ever experienced what they were feeling and thinking. The only difference between this couple and most baby boomers is that Adam and Eve were right—no one had experienced what they were experiencing. They believed the lie that there were no consequences to their actions and wanted to believe that their parent was the cause of the predicament. The serpent told them that God had lied to them about the consequences of their actions and that He only wanted to limit them. As baby boomers, we have learned the art of blaming our parents for our excesses and inadequacies. Without going into all of the theological ramifications of this story, it is quite evident that Adam and Eve wanted to be gods.

Is not the desire to be our own god the core flaw in all generations? We are no different than any other generation except that most of us have had the core watered and nourished by the culture in which we live. While we have frequently verbally acknowledged the existence and authority of God, our feelings, thoughts, and actions have denied it. We attended church, bought books, attended seminars, and purchased tapes, CDs, and DVDs to help us. But help us to do what? As much as we may not like to admit it, our deep desire is to be a better god.

While the self-help literature boom of the last 30 years may have helped a number of people make progress in specific issues of life, we might conclude that it has been a bust in helping humanity become well in quality and character. A gentleman whose bookstore was noted for its large section of self-help literature said that at times he felt guilty for his flagrant promotion of it. It was very profitable, he noted, but often those who purchased the most books were addicted to the subject rather than impacted by the material. He said, "Reading two self-help books apparently creates the illusion that you have really done something to help yourself."

But the soul flavored with humility realizes that while we make some improvement on our own, we can never be the superhuman we want to be. There is one God and that God alone is worthy of worship—all-powerful, unlimited, and all-knowing.

This truth may help us understand why Deuteronomy 6:4–9 was so important in family life during the Old Testament era:

> "Hear, O Israel: The LORD our God, the LORD is one. Love the LORD your God with all your heart and with all your soul and with all your strength. These commandments that I give you today are to be upon your hearts. Impress them on your children. Talk about them when you sit at home and when you walk along the road, when you lie down and when you get up. Tie them as symbols on your hands and bind them on your foreheads. Write them on the doorframes of your houses and on your gates."
>
> —Deuteronomy 6:4–9

Recognizing that there is only One who is God and that regardless of how much we improve we will never be God helps us to experience humility. A friend of mine is fond of saying that one of the reasons so many religious people are tired and miserable is that they are preparing themselves to be ready to fill in for God when He takes a day off or wants to go on vacation. Recognizing that we are not and never will be God is not a cross we carry; it is a crown that brings great joy in life.

The reason that many of us are emotionally and spiritually exhausted may not be because of our busy schedules but because of carrying the burden of trying to be god. At age 23, I heard a speaker ask the question, "Are you sick and tired of being sick and tired?" I remember thinking at the time that this was a question for losers who had given up. It was a question that I felt neither I nor people motivated like me would ever have to face or answer. Yet as I look over the last 10 years as a pastor of a large and diverse congregation, I realize that many of the high-energy achievers who would come to see me were frequently saying they were "sick and tired of being sick and tired." After one particular week of listening to the hurts of competent but wounded folks and seeing them leave disappointed that I could not wave the holy wand or give them the sacred lotion of prayer to make them feel better, I realized that I was sick and tired of being sick and tired. I was trying to be god to the people who were trying to be god, and we were all weary. Not only are more people in this generation professional caregivers than in any previous generation, but also we have great numbers of people who are performing the roles of caregiver without pay or credentials.

Because our generation has been blessed with affluence, we have assumed the role of financial caregiver to parents who are in nursing homes and places of extended care, while at the same time paying for kids in college. We are grateful that we have the means to shoulder such responsibility, but it is also a heavy burden to carry. As one 53-year-old who is quite successful said, "I have far exceeded my financial goals, but my financial responsibilities have also far exceeded my expectations. My aging mother, my single daughter with a child, my son in college, and the stockholders of my company are counting on me. I feel like everyone is expecting me to be god, and I realize that is what I am indirectly promising them." He is not so different from many other midlifers except that he recognizes his situation. How do we develop goodness when we are trying to live up to the responsibility of being god?

God Is God

The answer to this question is spiritual: we attempt to practice the first half of Psalm 46:10, which says, "Be still, and know that I am God." We locate a place where silence is prominent and have a spiritual retreat. We come back physically rested, but no more whole. A growing number in the 40 to 60 age group are taking spiritual retreats. Several non-profit executives have found it is very profitable to be CEOs of the organizations that own retreat centers. Providing a space and environment to get away for God is now an acceptable way of grabbing the gold. Yet being still does not guarantee that we will know that we are not God. Awareness that He is God often begins when we recognize the different areas of our life in which we are attempting to be God.

Here is a routine I learned from others and have found to be helpful. Each week, during my reflection time, I list the areas that I am trying to control and then through prayer release them. For example, during a building program in our church, we bumped into some major barriers that appeared they would keep us from completing the project on time. I had already announced to the church one major delay and I did not want to sing the second verse of the "I Am Sorry to Inform You" hymn. I began to put pressure on the staff member and committee responsible for providing leadership on this project, knowing they would in turn apply pressure to the companies involved. In spite of my "encouragement," which sounds much more acceptable than "pressure," we found that the delay in completing the project was even worse than our worst case scenario.

Frustrated and fuming, I spent my time trying to figure out how we could leverage this into lowering our cost, ways I could word this to the church that did not make me look bad, and what I could do to recover from an imagined public relations issue within

> *Awareness that He is God often begins when we recognize the different areas of our life in which we are attempting to be God.*

The Value of Humility

the church. During my reflection time I became aware that I was trying to play god with this and wanted to give the appearance of being all powerful as senior pastor to the church. I, along with staff and the lay committee members, had done all that we could do. All we could say to the church was, "In spite of our best efforts, the building will not be completed on the last date projected. We hope but do not guarantee that it will be completed by..."

Often we are attempting to be god in our family issues as well. An acquaintance of mine has been very frustrated with his son in college. The young man apparently approached his time at the university like a mass murderer does prison; he assumed it was for life, therefore there was never a need to hurry. He changed majors several times, he took the minimum number of hours to be considered a full-time student, and he spent more hours each week playing video games than he did attending class. The father had not only threatened to stop paying the bills, he also delivered on the threat. The son, much to the father's dismay, had qualified for a loan and had figured how he could stay in school three more semesters before he had to start repaying any of the loans.

My acquaintance was losing sleep at night. He prayed that God would give him the wisdom and knowledge to know what to say to spark a fire in the young man's ambition. During his prayer time he realized that even though he and his wife had been God's biological instruments to bring the young man into existence, they were not his creator, sustainer, and redeemer. He said recognizing this fact was not what he thought of as humbling, but freeing. He could let God work in his son's life and if his son chose to reject God's leadership, it was tragic, but he did not have to feel like he had rejected God. This is humility. Humility begins with recognizing you are not God.

As we begin to release areas of our life to God, we also need to repent of our failed but determined attempts to be god. We would like to think that lack of humility is just an inevitable stage of life and not a character flaw. As a result, we think of repenting of a lack of humility as being similar to repenting of puberty. We did not ask for it, so why do we need to apologize for it?

Repentance

Repentance is a word and concept that seems harsh. It was a word that folks of the G.I. Joe generation used regularly in their religious experiences. Repentance slipped out the back door when self-esteem walked in the front door. When Karl Menninger wrote his classic *Whatever Became of Sin?* he reintroduced the issue of repentance. While the church culture was moving away from the word, the larger society was moving away from the entire concept.

Repentance is acknowledging that we are responsible and that our irresponsible actions have been directed toward God and toward individuals created in God's image. The act of repentance, of confessing and turning away from our sin, not only indicates that humility exists as a character trait; it also enlarges, expands, and elevates humility.

Confession is good for the soul and is the first step toward repentance. The initial discomfort of confession is more than compensated by the cleansing that results. But that cleansing has the life of a three-year-old farm boy's bath—it's gone soon after sunrise.

For the past few years, I have attempted to write out my prayers of repentance. It's difficult to fully explain, but something happens to me in the process of writing out my confessions. I find that in writing, I am more specific. Perhaps more importantly, seeing the words in print keeps them from evaporating into air the way they do after I have spoken them. The written repentance not only makes my confession more tangible and observable, it also helps me to realize that my sins are real and tangible; they do harm and damage in reality. By keeping these words in a prayer journal that I review at least once a month, I am continually aware that my sins are not just occasional acts of aberrant behavior, but patterns that can be observed at any stage of my life.

If I spend too much time in reviewing my lists of sins, it can become morbid and depressing. Therefore, I also write down words acknowledging my awareness of God's forgiveness. Repenting helps humility to move beyond just a feeling to be imprinted in our soul and work itself into the DNA of our spirit. Repentance is both the practice and promotion of humility.

Humility and Others

Humility is not a virtue that is only practiced in the privacy of one's soul; it must be a component that is plugged into our relationship network. If we are good, genuinely and authentically good in character, humility will impact the way we interact with those around us.

I don't mind feigning humility when it works for me, but I also like to use the mirage of invincibility when it helps me get what I want. I doubt that I am different than most folks my age. A very senior adult recently told me that he found that he could connect much better with his adult grandchildren than he could with his own baby boomer children. He said, "My adult grandchildren were obnoxious as teenagers, but they got over it in college. My baby boomer children and their friends never got over it. Don't take this personally, but you baby boomers are never wrong. When baby boomers are wrong, they just change the rules and make it right." Then he was kind enough to suggest that I was the exception and did not match the common profile of my generation. I lived up to my generation's values first by thinking he was right in his evaluation of me and then that he was wrong in his evaluation of the rest of my peers.

Yet this sage may be on to something about us. The divorce rate has stayed high as we have aged, and our passion for litigation has moved attorneys ahead of physicians as the profession of privilege and ridicule. Not only does our generation divorce more often, in our watch we have seen the "no fault" divorce emerge because or our refusal to admit the possibility that we are wrong. We do have a difficult time admitting moral wrong, and we will spare no cost to society to prove that we are not wrong. On the political stage we have heard the language "Don't ask, don't tell" that will protect folks from having to make a moral judgment that could be questioned.

The refusal to admit error has entered churches and community organizations. In our generation, there are more splits in churches than in bowling alleys, and frequently the split is sanctified as church growth. In one major southern city, two churches were honored by their denominations and publicized in the media for being two of the fastest growing churches in the nation. Yet both of them were split-offs from existing churches that became two of the fastest declining churches in the nations. Even the not-for-profit corporations that we created to do good and to compensate for our greed have frequently been divided because the philanthropic founders could give away everything except their passion to always be right and never admit wrong.

A Character Audit

Humility not only keeps us from thinking we are gods, it also keeps us from assuming that we are superior among those we label, for public relations purposes, as equals. One of the best ways to find our whether your humility is a reality or a mirage is to develop a way of finding out what others really think about you. I know of one man who does a character audit every three years. Although his method is very expensive and thorough, he feels it is worth the expense and effort because he is a better man and his company is a better organization. He meets with his accountants and gives them a list of one hundred business associates, competitors, colleagues, church leaders, and friends who interact with him. He then asks his accountants to choose 20 to send character evaluations to, assuring those filling out the questionnaire that their identity will not be known to him. His accounting firm can also send the evaluation to people not on the list if they feel that he has packed the list with folks who will give him a favorable rating. The first time he used this evaluation, he scored very low in the virtue of humility. This surprised him, and he asked his wife if that was a fair evolution and she confirmed that he had honest and perceptive friends. During the last six years, he has deliberately attempted to express more humility in his professional and personal relationships. He says that expressing humility has made him more humble in character. It is not the "fake it until you make it" concept, but is more the "actions produce attitude" concept.

While this gentleman obviously had the resources to do a thorough character audit, those with lesser financial means can certainly apply and downsize the methods he used to meet their circumstances. We are not usually good judges of the quality of our humility because most of us battle the demon of insecurity, which we often mistakenly assume is identical to humility. Insecurity is a vice that allows us to tell ourselves we are humble while creating the image of an angry victim. Self-centered creatures will inevitably suffer the twin plagues of insecurity and the appearance of overconfidence. Because of the emphasis on self, we feel inadequate and compensate by acting as if we are very sure in ourselves. Not only does this explain why humility is lacking, but it also helps us to understand why humility does not even appear on the screen when we download our want list. Methods to find and analyze the degree of humility that is evident in our life will need to involve others.

While accountability groups definitely help with this, the small chosen group has some inherent weaknesses when diagnosing humility deficiencies. One of the dirty little secrets of the small group accountability movement is that it can lead to an inflated sense of pride. Please do not read this as indictment on gathering in small groups for examination regarding issues of the soul. But because the small group method has become the primary means of moral and spiritual accountability in the last 20 years, participants can begin to feel superior because they are in an accountability group. This immediately minimizes the role that virtue plays in their lives. Surveys and questionnaires, which are often perceived as only tools of the academic and marketing communities, can be excellent means of examining the humility factor.

Because of the emphasis on self, we feel inadequate and compensate by acting as if we are very sure in ourselves.

At 45 years of age, a businesswoman who 10 years earlier began a fast and upward climb on the success ladder began to sense distance between her and the people who had helped her ascend to the top. She developed a brief five-question questionnaire for friends. She asked them to evaluate her moral and spiritual strengths and areas of potential growth and gave them some specific questions to aid in the process. Obviously these good friends wrote many positive things, but they also indicated that her confidence sometimes appeared to cross over the line into the dangerous zone of arrogance. This helped her understand that the old statement of conventional wisdom, "it is lonely at the top," does not always emanate from professional jealousy, but can also be stimulated by a dearth of humility. As result, she no longer assumed that the solution to her loneliness was social networking but realized that it was the character issue of humility.

Other attempts at improvement in humility are simple, including articles and books about humility in a scheduled reading plan. Almost all of Henri Nouwen's works eventually lead to the issue of humility. One man I know who appears to balance financial success, political influence, and character as well as anyone makes it a point to read Nouwen on a regular basis, even though he differs theologically and politically with him.

Still another way is to have someone you trust occasionally read your daily journal. This introduces the element of risk because you definitely need to trust the person reading your letters from the soul. But risk is directly related to humility. People who are afraid to risk are often fearful of finding out they were wrong. Acknowledging sin and error is the antecedent of grace. The heart lacking in humility will always trade well being for grace.

Humility Listens

Perhaps the most effective exercise in bringing shape to the humility muscles of the soul is the practice of listening. Listening is both a cause and result of humility. In several chapters in this book, the issue of listening is mentioned. While listening is important to every generation, it is very important to baby boomers, because in our lifetime we have seen the shift to visual communication. We have learned as adults that presentations to groups without using PowerPoint is like having a birthday party without a birthday cake. It can happen, but it doesn't seem right.

As a result, we have worked on presentation skills, trying to figure how to connect images and words so that people can get the message we want them to experience. Yet we have forgotten that communication is a two-way street, and while we have paved the talk lane, we have allowed the listen lane to become a gravel path. Listening works on the following humility assumption: the other person has a contribution to make to our lives. If we do not think we have a need or the other person can meet that need, we will not listen. Really listening makes us aware of our own inadequacy.

Within the last year, I had a conference with a young lady regarding a decision about a career change. She was asking permission to use my name as a reference and for advice regarding networking with folks who could open doors for her in the new profession. We did the normal small talk routine about her family, my family, and what was happening in our church. I released all the wisdom I had stored behind the maturity door and our meeting was concluded.

Later that evening, I realized that during the small talk I had asked her about her efforts in one ministry area of our church and that she had given me a negative response. She had essentially said in very kind words that this ministry was not getting it done, and I had nodded and gone onto the next question.

Later, I realized her insight was profound. Why did I choose to ignore her insight? There were several reasons. First, I was not expecting an evaluation in response to my question; I was anticipating that this question would only lead to more small talk. Second, I had never considered this young lady as making a conceptual contribution to the church. Third, I was anxious to share my insights about her career changes because not only did I know several people in that profession who could be helpful to her, but also I perceived myself to be knowledgeable in that area. The bottom line was that my arrogance caused me to miss the wisdom of her insight.

> *Listening is difficult for people who think they are special.*

I scheduled a second appointment with her, and this time I listened. I learned a great deal not only about this ministry but also about how some minor changes in my leadership style could help this ministry not only survive but thrive.

Listening is difficult for people who think they are special. A mother of the bride told me that, after her daughter's wedding, there was a continuing amount of stress in the family. When I asked why, she said, "When my daughter was getting married, we told her that this was a special event in her life. This wedding was one occasion for her to make choices based solely on her preferences. She did not need to take into account the desires of anyone else because this was her day. She followed our instructions, and as a family, we made certain there was not one affordable wish that we did not fulfill. But now my daughter has failed to realize the wedding is over and she is no longer a bride but now a married woman. She still expects us to do what she wants. She no longer listens to any of our preferences, but acts like every day is her wedding day. She is still hearing the wedding march and hasn't realized the organist has stopped playing."

Change the details and this could be the story of an entire generation of people who have difficulty listening. The Scripture says where there is no vision the people perish, but it might also be said that where there is no listening, character perishes.

CHAPTER 9

The Action
of Celebration

The Isley Brothers Got It Right—
Just "Shout"

RE VIRTUES THE ONLY INGREDIENTS in the good life? Virtues are important ingredients, but there is at least one holy action required. While occasionally some have called it a virtue, it appears to be more of a catalyst that helps to start the virtue-driven life.

A successful high school basketball coach surprised his players, their parents, and the fans in his district when he unexpectedly announced, after winning the state championship, that he was leaving the coaching profession at the age of 47 to open his own business. The motivating factor for his decision was not the desire to leave the low salaries of public education or the weariness of living in the proverbial "glass house" of coaching, having all your actions evaluated by fans. He said the primary reason was that highs were not as high as they once were and the lows were lower than they used to be. This was an interesting and revealing admission after experiencing the pinnacle of success in his profession. It was as if he could no longer hear the applause and only took note of the flaws.

When the Thrill Is Gone

Authors, counselors, movie produces, and songwriters have frequently addressed the issue of what happens in relationships after time has passed and the romance turns into routine. Perhaps the Eagles said it best in "After the Thrill Is Gone" with these words:

The flame rises but it soon descends
Empty pages and a frozen pen
You're not quite lovers and you're not quite friends

The increased divorce rate among baby boomers tells us that living longer does not mean everything automatically improves with age. Some relationships rot while others ferment. The idiosyncrasies that once attracted them become what they despise in each other. Once they experienced nightly passion in the bedroom and celebration on the weekend. They celebrated promotions, raises, buying their first home, the arrival of the first child, and the first steps and first words of their progeny. But then, over the years, there were fewer firsts and more feelings of "been there and done that."

Husbands and wives at midlife go their separate ways and connect with other people, expecting to find something new, only to realize that the thrill was not so much with the other person as it was with the stage of life. There is some anecdotal evidence that many couples who divorce for the first time in their 40s are more likely to divorce again in their 50s as well. The issue of losing the "thrill" is much larger than marriage. In fact, it may be the primary midlife issue. Four decades of living can deplete thrill and the thrill reserves and leave you with the feeling that there is nothing left to celebrate.

Several factors may contribute to this absence of celebration in life. By the time we reach 40 years of age, we have fewer and fewer new experiences. We find that innovation has been replaced with tradition, and we are only repeating past events. It is difficult to celebrate what has become routine.

If we bought into the baby boomer myth that life was always going to get better and better, then what happens when life becomes demythologized? Some place along the way, we find out that we carry the moniker of being "an average person." Perish the thought! At age 44, we know we will no longer be the young rising star in the organization, and our goal is no longer stardom but survival. Although we never wanted to ruin any other person's marriage, we do not want to be seen as the office eunuch either. Is surviving as a genuinely nice guy or a matronly—albeit a sharply dressed and younger matronly—woman any reason to celebrate?

A vice president in a large banking organization told me that at age 45 his career path had been written in stone. He knew that there was nothing he could do to ever rise beyond what had been slotted for him. But he did know that a major misstep in financial judgment or significant faux pas in office politics could cause him to be pushed off his midlevel rung of the corporate ladder. He said, "I celebrate each December 31 that I have not been fired, but asking my wife to go out to nice restaurant to celebrate that seems like a waste of both our time."

Needless to say, his celebration potential seemed rather small to him. I once asked him when was the last time he and his wife had celebrated anything other than a birthday or anniversary, and he could not remember. The skyscrapers and suburbs are full of these people who feel they have no reason to celebrate. They are all dressed up with possessions and positions their parents would have died for, but they feel like they have nothing to celebrate.

Defeating Cynicism

Another reason it is difficult to celebrate at midlife is that we may have caved into the temptation of being cynical. It is the attitude disease that is very likely to strike about the age of 40 and has been known to be fatal to the human spirit. We have learned the hard way that not all of life is what it appears to be. We have seen politicians, religious leaders, community power brokers, and media personalities fail. We begin to think that all people who are thought to have good character are just those who have, as yet, not been caught.

Cynics perceive that goodness is an illusion of the naïve. We have watched as the good guys wearing the white hats were discovered to be bad guys who found a place to get their hats cleaned. We have done good deeds only to see them used against us. Now we know why our curmudgeon uncle had the epitaph "No good deed goes unpunished" carved on his tombstone.

It is difficult to celebrate when you are cynical because you suspiciously think that everyone who is celebrating is faking it. The media viewing habits for many baby boomers have stimulated and fueled cynicism. Two television programs filled our homes with laughter as we were working through the first half of life, and also may have shaped our minds, attitudes, and our souls more than we would like to admit. Both *M.A.S.H* and *Seinfeld* were considered necessary entertainment for ambitious people who wanted to fit in with the culture. These were not only filled with witty repartee but also with cynicism.

A television series about the Korean War packaged to attract those who struggled with the Vietnam War, *M.A.S.H.* portrayed all authority figures as either being corrupt or painfully naïve. Commanding officers were to be disobeyed because they just didn't get it, and the well-intentioned but bumbling priest was a figure to be pitied. The character Hawkeye Pierce distrusted every institution and his suspicions were proven right at the end of the 30-minute episode.

Seinfeld made humorous heroes and heroines out of despicable characters who lied, lusted, and cheated their way through every situation. This sarcastic but hilarious sitcom has so impacted our culture that we now use words in daily conversation that were either first used or popularized by *Seinfeld*. Say "Yada, yada, yada" and "Festivus" and even people who don't know their origins will understand the cynical under-pinnings of the words.

While cynicism has always been a staple humor of intellectuals, we have been the first generation that has seen cynical humor popularized as the most common of entertainment for the commoners. I confess that the popularity of cynicism has greatly impacted my writing and speaking style. Cynics get heard. The media has done to cynicism what Wal-Mart did with merchandise—made it available to everyone and convinced them that they needed it. Most cynics only celebrate when they find out that their prediction that it would rain on someone's parade was accurate. Cynics feel that if they celebrate for any other reason, then they have sold out.

Celebration and Character

So what's wrong with abstinence from celebration and why does celebration have anything to do with character? You may be wondering who made celebration a holy action that is a necessary ingredient for character anyway. *Character* conjures up images of disciplines that are unpleasant and acquired tastes. *Character* reminds you of vegetables, vitamins, and sugar-free candy. Someone has told you that if you consume them long enough, you will learn to like them, but people lie about many things.

Celebration brings to mind music, dancing, chocolate, and laughter. For many midlifers there appears to be a disconnect between character and celebration. This disconnect is the result of our misunderstanding of the nature of celebration, the biblical message, and how people with character really live.

The verb "to celebrate" is connected to the idea of frequenting or repeating. It is the idea of reliving a good event by creating an event in its honor. Celebration is more like a living symbol or a holy action than a virtue. It is for this reason that liturgical churches speak of celebrating the Eucharist, and evangelicals speak of celebrating baptism. Neither of these religious events is put in the category of a New Year's Eve gig with party hats and whoopee cushions, but these sacred events are both in keeping with the real meaning of celebrating in that we remember or relive past events with festivities.

Both the call and the commission to celebrate are rooted firmly in the Old Testament. One of the more frequent commands given to God's people in the Old Testament is to celebrate. This may surprise the modern Christian because we often perceive the God described in the Old Testament as similar to the deity Jonathan Edwards portrayed in his sermon "Sinners in the Hands of an Angry God."

A careful reading of the first 39 books of the Bible reveals God instituting many feasts and holy days designed to break the daily routine of life and allow people in a very harsh world to have some joyous experiences. The concept of Jubilee is foreign to most of us, yet it was commanded in the Old Testament. In the Year of Jubilee, people were released from indebtedness, the planting of crops was forbidden, and even slaves were set free. While there were many social implications of the Year of Jubilee, including a form of redistribution of wealth, the reason was to celebrate God's goodness. They were remembering how God had provided in years past and therefore confident that He would provide in the future. If we had Jubilee today, it would be more anticipated than Christmas, your birthday, the Super Bowl, and New Years Day combined.

> *In the Year of Jubilee, people were released from indebtedness, the planting of crops was forbidden, and even slaves were set free.*

These Old Testament holy days are forerunners to what we now call holidays and time off. While our society moves to a more secular calendar and wants to no longer acknowledge the religious connections to the holidays, we do not hear anyone calling for our society to forgo the holidays. Instead, we hear government leaders, labor unions, and public opinion polls advocating that we observe more legal holidays. We want the "holi"-day without the "holy," and yet the very nature of holidays is firmly grounded in the holy nature of God.

One reason we have difficulty seeing celebration as a commanded holy action is because of the way holiday celebrations have changed in the last 50 years. Historically, celebrations were occasions set aside for the purpose of remembering past significant events. The holy season of Passover was for remembering God's great act of redemption. At Christmas we remember Jesus's birth, and at Easter we remember

His resurrection. This was true for secular holidays as well. Independence Day was to remember our nation's freedom. Memorial Day was set aside to honor those who had died in war. Veteran's Day was established to remember the sacrifices of those who had served in the military in times of war.

We are seeing some needed changes in corporate worship practices, but not all the changes are necessarily healthy. For example, worship is often called a celebration just because the music is upbeat, the preacher dresses casually, and choirs with long robes and long faces have been replaced with perky smiling praise teams clothed by The Gap. But for worship to be celebration, it must help us remember the mighty acts of God throughout the ages and in the last week. Both traditional and contemporary worship forms in our generation appear to be answering the question of "How do I make it to Friday?" Both the Sabbath in the Old Testament and the Lord's Day in the New Testament were celebrations advocating remembering and reciting the works of a holy, living God, which in turn gives hope that there will be a Friday and an eternity.

The New Testament also presents celebration as a character virtue. As Richard Foster reminds us in his book *Celebration of Discipline,* Jesus entered and exited the world under a silver-lined cloud of celebration. In Luke 2:10 an angel marked the event with these words, "Do not be afraid. I bring you good news of great joy that will be for all the people." Then Jesus, in His pre-cross farewell, said, "I have told you this so that my joy may be in you and that your joy may be complete" (John 15:11).

This does not sound like "With heads bowed and eyes closed, let's sing more verses, and if no one comes we will then decide what to do next." This sounds more like "Ladies and gentlemen, start your engines because the wonderful race of life is about to begin." In fact, Jesus even chided His opponents who apparently criticized Jesus for too much celebration and indicated they preferred the more conservative John the Baptist. Foster notes 12 historic disciplines and places "celebration" as the first of the corporate disciplines. Long before baby boomers arrived, holy hopeful people saw the need for celebration. The road to good character is always paved with celebration.

Why Celebrate?

The first response of many who are informed of the need to celebrate is "Why?" Other virtues even sound religious. Who could argue with humility, gratefulness, community, forgiveness, relationship, and solitude? But celebration appears on the surface to be one of those nice but not absolutely necessary character traits, sort of like "National Be Kind to Plumbers Day." If you could miss only one session in character formation class, it might appear that the day they lectured on celebration might be a good time to get your teeth cleaned. Celebration is more than a good option. It is essential in building character that will not crash and fail under the pressure of the last half of your life.

Celebration may not be the mother of all character, but she is definitely a family member. Celebration will change our attitude toward life, others, ourselves, and

God, as well as help us desire the necessary virtues. Celebration provides the perspective and emotional energy to engage in the search for goodness for goodness' sake. Character building is not for the weak and faint of heart. Celebration is the high energy drink for thirsty souls that provides strength and stamina for the long but wonderful journey.

Those who celebrate begin not by evaluating or tracking what has happened in their lives but by studying the goodness of God. They begin the process by looking at life through faith-colored glasses. To celebrate means to look at the life we have been given and say it is good.

This does not mean we should pretend that life is always comfortable, easy, or pleasant. But as believers in the Lord Jesus Christ, we know that our past has been forgiven, our present is directed by the Holy Spirit, and we are anticipating the reality of eternal life. Isn't that a reason to celebrate? Sure there is hurt, harm, and disappointment in life, but as the sanctified bumper sticker says, "Stuff happens." The Merry Melodies cartoons that we grew up with usually concluded with "Th- th- th- that's all, folks." As people of faith we know that line, even without the stutter, can never be delivered. We have hope until there is no more love left in Jesus.

Two of my grandparents greatly influenced my life, and mostly for good. Although both were active in their churches and came from the rural Missouri Ozarks, they had totally opposite approaches to life.

My father's mother was one of the most determined people that I ever met. By the time she was 35, she was providing for seven children and an invalid husband. During the prohibition era, she turned neighbors in to the county sheriff for "moonshining," and five days later, she watched helplessly as her house burned to the ground. Law authorities told her they were certain they knew who was behind the arson, but they could not prove it in court. When she was elderly and I was eight years old, I asked her if she regretted calling the authorities on her bootlegger neighbors. She said that she had no regrets and would do it again.

In her 46th year, she lost two teenage daughters to influenza, a seven-year-old son in a hunting accident, and her husband after his long health battle ended in death. Yet in the most painful year of her life, she did not crumble or break. Her surviving children said the events that year made her more determined than ever. I remember my grandmother as a woman who would fight injustice regardless of who was inflicting it, even if it was her pastor or a law enforcement officer.

For two years she lived with my parents, my older brother, and me. During the day, she provided sole care for me as both parents worked and my brother was in school. I knew as long as she was with me I did not need to be afraid of anyone. Although I knew no one else would harm me, at times I was not sure I could survive her intense stare when I disobeyed her or challenged her opinion. I am convinced her stare could have made O. J. confess, Charles Manson cry, and Osama Bin Laden surrender. People frequently spoke their admiration for her, but I do not know of any close friends she had.

My mother's father was completely the opposite. He would rather laugh than work and always knew the latest clean joke. When I was small, he would teach me the meanings of jokes and also how to tell these jokes to adults in order to impress them. He knew that humor was in the timing. Even now, whenever I deliver the punch line just right on Sunday morning and hear the laughter, I think of my grandfather.

> *Even now, whenever I deliver the punch line just right on Sunday morning and hear the laughter, I think of my grandfather.*

If there was enough food on the table and most of the bills were paid, he felt that he had provided well for his family. He was not afraid of hard work if it was absolutely necessary, but the operative word was "absolutely." He was known to have taken days off for no other reason than that he felt like it. When he retired, he walked each day to the town square and interacted with the people he met on the street. He always came home with a new funny story. He enjoyed lemon drop candy and Beeswax chewing tobacco, and frequently he simultaneously kept a lemon drop in the left side of his mouth and a very small wad of tobacco in the right side. When asked why he had both in his mouth at the same time, he would reply, "Life is too short not to enjoy the good things."

I remember hearing his laughter when he entered our house. He would pick me up as long as he had the health and the strength to lift me. When he lost his wife of 48 years, I saw him weep for the first time. I remember walking onto the front porch of his house the day my grandmother died. He picked me up and said, "Young man, you appear to need a lemon drop." Even in the drab and dreary nursing home where he spent his last 11 months, you could hear his laughter down the hall. He was loved by almost everyone except a couple of workaholic sons-in-law, but as far as I know, he was no one's hero, only everyone's friend.

While I benefited from both grandparents and they both obviously left a positive imprint on my life, I have enjoyed life and influenced others most when I was more like my grandfather. For years I thought of grandfather more as charming gadfly than a man with character, but as I grow older I see that he was man of authentic character. Yes, he had his flaws, but he really saw life as a gift and everyday as an occasion to celebrate. His face will never be on Mount Rushmore, and I don't think he was ever nominated to serve on the church board, although he was frequently bored at church. Yet, he enjoyed and celebrated life. When I do let my hair down and deliberately seek to emulate his characteristics, I have the most influence on my family and friends.

My tendency is to be more like my grandmother than my grandfather. I have been known to rain on people's parades in the name of making sure things are done right. I have chided when people needed cheering, and in the pursuit of excellence, I have pushed people into mediocrity. Christian celebration recognizes that while not everything is done right, we can do the right things, and celebrating is doing the right thing.

Celebration Is Contagious

Folks who celebrate also motivate. People of good character desire to influence others, and it is through celebration that we inspire and influence. Being told 50 times each day to have a good attitude does not build good attitude. People who celebrate life create a positive and good attitude within us.

The postmodern thinkers and emergent church leaders are combining to tell us that our method of religious teaching has been too heavy on the teacher talk and student listen mode rather than upon the concept of teacher and student experiencing truth together, engaging in dialogue. The mentor method of teaching historically has proven superior to the classroom approach to teaching character. A person who celebrates will always attract people. Their spirit is contagious. People who do not celebrate limit their sphere of influence because people will not want to be around them. Good people influence people to be and do good.

I live in Alabama, a place where college football is almost a religion, and in fact, the athletic departments are far better supported through charitable donations than most churches. Both of our major college football programs, the University of Alabama and Auburn University, have a rich and storied tradition. At different times in the last few years, each school has suffered under sanctions by the NCAA, the governing body of college athletics. As a result, each school has had at least one three-year period in which their records have been less than stellar. Both teams always sell all of their tickets, but I know the kind of year they are having by the number of free tickets people offer to me or to our church staff. In the lean years, church members will generously offer their tickets to the staff. One year a fan offered his four season tickets to any staff member.

But during my tenure, each team also has had one perfect season. Fans did not offer me their tickets during these 13–0 seasons. I think some would have rather parted with their firstborn than to give up their tickets to watch their team win. These folks are not just alumni who enjoy a Saturday back at their alma mater. Many went to other schools but over the years have enjoyed being associated with winning football traditions. They enjoy celebrating after the game more than the game itself.

> People who do not celebrate limit their sphere of influence because people will not want to be around them. Good people influence people to be and do good.

Winning and celebrating go together. People who are perceived to be winners in life attract others. This sounds like you have to have a perfect season of life in order to influence people, but this is not so. As believers in Jesus Christ, we are already winners. Our winning is not the result of our perfection but because of grace and hope. Few people realize we are winners because they do not see us celebrating in our lives. Character is not about faking celebration in order to influence people. It is recognizing that at all times and in all circumstances there are reasons for celebrating.

I do personal business in the offices of a local financial institution three or four times each year. The person who handles my account has an infectious smile and contagious laugh. Instead of "hello," she generally says, "Isn't it a fantastic day?" when you enter her office. On one occasion she excused herself to take a cell phone call, and when she returned the smile was less vibrant and there was a look of concern on her face. I asked if everything was alright and she replied that she was dealing with some medical decisions regarding her husband's cancer. The latest method of treatment was not providing the desired result, and they were deciding if they should continue the treatment. Before I could utter a caring cliché she said, "We are people of faith and we are going to make it, regardless of what happens, so I choose to think about my daily victories rather than the defeats. Would you like to hear about the fantastic grades my daughter made in her first year of college?" The smile returned and there was an upward turn in her voice.

During the first 40 years of our life, we generally celebrate our successes and moments of significance. When we have accomplished a goal or have reached a new level of recognition, we celebrate. Now at midlife, our successes appear to be fewer and we realize that our significance is not what we thought it was.

As we honestly reflect on the achievements and the events we have celebrated in times past, we realize that many of our trophies were given more as the result of our combination of luck, ego, greed, and ignorance than of excellence. At midlife, we have the capacity to celebrate far more worthy things than doing well; we can celebrate the goodness of God and of His people.

A CEO who founded his own company in his late 20s was asked to identify his most significant success for a feature article about him in business journal. While thinking through the question, he said that he would have answered that question differently in every decade.

He said at age 30 his answer would have been founding his own company. At age 40 his answer would have been the great financial success that came as the result of entering the international market. But at age 50, he realized that he stumbled on the plan for the company through the help of college buddies, and it was not so much of an accomplishment as it was luck. The same could be said of the decision to go international with his product because his accountant and his wife put great pressure on him to make that move based on a hunch. He said, "Much of what I accomplished has been as a result of being lucky, but one thing that is not the result of luck is the integrity we have built into this organization. I have had to ter-minate friends from the company, and at times pro-mote some folks whose hard questions became irritating, but I determined that I would rather fail than give any appearance of deception and dishonesty. My greatest accomplishment is the paragraph that has been in our auditor's report each year regarding integrity."

Celebration is directly related to how we keep score. A bumper sticker that originated during the 1980s has rightly been the subject of many negative articles, speeches, and books. It has been worded several ways, but the last version I saw was on the back bumper of a BMW and read: "He who has the most toys at the end wins." Obviously, this is a materialistic view of life. However, many who would die before they would paste that sticker on their bumper keep score the same way. When we are in the process of determining what is really important and what is not, then we may discover we have far more to celebrate than when we thought money, sex, and power were the only ways we could keep score. At midlife, we find that the dream of being rich is never going to be achieved, sex is more of a process than an event, and power was what we used to think we had, but if we have integrity we have reason to celebrate.

> *At midlife, we have the capacity to celebrate far more worthy things than doing well; we can celebrate the goodness of God and of His people.*

Life is a wonderful mystery, and if the cynicism of adulthood derails our journey through the land of awe, we are headed in the wrong direction. The definition of *awe* is "rapt attention and deep emotion caused by the sight of something extraordinary." As a child growing up in an emotionally healthy home, the awe is inevitable. But in the adult world of budgets, bricks, barriers, bombs, and bother, we have to deliberately work at keeping the awe in sight. Optimism and positive thinking are two wonderful attributes, but they may be symptoms more than causes. People who celebrate will be optimistic and have a positive attitude because they are not only practicing goodness, they are also promoting it.

Steps to Celebration

But how do you deliberately weave celebration into your life? While there is not a specific formula for celebration, there are some basics.

First, remember celebrations require a break in routine. We celebrate holy days and holidays by changing our routine. At Christmas, offices close, we exchange gifts, and we gather with family and friends. We do not do that on June 9 or October 3, but we do on and around December 25.

By midlife we have learned our routines and may find that it is difficult to change. You can experience celebration by going to a new restaurant, attending a sporting or music event that normally you would not, or worshiping in a different religious setting. A couple with whom I am acquainted had gone to the beach for 25 consecutive years and it became as routine as going to work. One year, this couple chose to take a week and work on a summer mission project with a group people from another church instead of going to the beach. It was a life changing experience for them. They have told friends and family members it is the event that delivered him out of the midlife malaise that was on the fast track to becoming depression.

Second, avoid analyzing the motives for the actions of others. Our generation had the scientific method deeply engraved into our learning process. When you combine the emphasis on empirical proof prominent in the scientific method with Freud, you want to find a cause behind everyone's actions, including your own. Much of the pop psychology that forms the story line for television and movies is based on discovering why people do what they do. It is even more devastating when we move this linear cause-and-effect thinking into evaluating why God does what He does. If you can explain the actions of God through cause and effect, you eliminate grace.

After failures, we are quick to ask, "Why did I do that?" and then seek non-existent answers. It is difficult to celebrate life when you are constantly questioning motives, because you will eventually ask the question, "Why am I celebrating?" Yes, we are all selfish and self-centered people who do things that benefit us and occasionally do altruistic actions. For once, rather than finding the log in your brother's eye or in your own, close your eyes and celebrate the miracle of sight and insight.

Third, find out the good events in others' lives and celebrate them. Often the real essence of celebrating is when we celebrate for and with others. This not only builds character, it *is* character. A man who has just entered the second half of his first century takes each of his employees out to lunch on or around their tenth, twentieth, and thirtieth wedding anniversaries. His lunch sometimes inspires some of the husbands to do more than they had planned on to celebrate their own anniversary. He inevitably goes home more appreciative of his own marriage. A schoolteacher in Birmingham sends a gift immediately on hearing that one of her colleagues is going to be a grandmother for the first time. She said shopping for the gifts brings back the feeling of the joy she had when her grandchildren were born.

Fourth, experience the value of corporate worship. When Christians gather for worship on Sundays, we are practicing the virtue of celebration. Church attendance and participation that only flows from duty fails to meet the celebration character requirement. But when we enter the worship center with the deliberate intention of rehearing and retelling the mighty acts of God, we are making progress on the journey toward goodness.

I have attended church regularly all my life. My parents required church attendance when I was young, and now my employer does. The church I serve as pastor has the expectation that I should not only attend but participate every Sunday.

But participating in a worship service in the draught-damaged country of Malawi changed my understanding of worship. In a poor and AIDS-decimated village where the life expectancy had dropped 14 years in the last two decades, I sat on the platform and watched people arrive for a worship experience. Bare feet, malnourished bodies, and decaying teeth could be seen all over the room. During the two-hour service, the people expressed their worship through music, dance, and tears.

When the service was over and the people were leaving, their expressions and their actions were different than when they arrived. There were more smiles and they did not appear to be forced, but were the result of hope. We walked with our host pastor back to his small residence and ate with his family. The floor was dirt and the walls were partially mud and rock. A portion of the meal was served with bare hands, and then we blessed the food as we joined hands.

After the meal, the pastor and his wife took us on a walking tour of the village. He pointed out where many of the people in his congregation lived, and frequently they came to the doors of their huts and with bright smiles engaged us in conversation. Most of the people who were not part of his or any congregation would not look us in the face, and when they did we could see the despair in their eyes. The expressions on their faces were much different than those of the people who had been in church. I asked him if he had trained the believers to smile. He said, "People who worship have hope, therefore they can smile. You will find the smiles gradually diminishing by the end of the week. On Sunday the smiles are reborn." Worship reminds us we have hope, and hope makes us smile.

In the U.S., we have Bible studies, seminars, and televised church, but nothing builds hope like corporate worship. The power is not in the music and not in the preaching. It is in the gathering with God's people and retelling and rehearsing the mighty acts of God. If a generation leaves worship out of their routine, it will not be long until celebration is absent from their character. Without worship, the virtues become rules by which we keep score rather than disciplines that help us become good for goodness' sake.

CHAPTER 10

Finding the On-Ramp on the Journey to Goodness

EYNOLDS WAS AN ELDERLY GENTLEMAN who, on his good days, was considered unpleasant by his neighbors and on most days was a cantankerous old codger you tried to avoid. We lived in the same neighborhood during the late 1970s. For a reason we never understood, he fell in love with our dachshund and would let him have the run of his house. Daily he cooked a patty of ground round for the dog and even asked if I would sell him our kid's pooch.

Because of his love for our dog, I was one of the few people with whom he would visit. He frequently complained about the misery of retirement. He and his wife lived in an ample but not luxurious home. Their house was beautifully placed on a waterfront lot that allowed them to view their private boat dock and professionally landscaped flower garden. By the time I met him, he had been retired for ten years and in spite of what appeared to be the good life, he exuded toxic discontent. He was reminiscent of the spoiled rich kid who, instead of enjoying the posh summer camp his parents paid for, perceives it to be a form of punishment. Reynolds said his wife told him daily that he had the retirement most folks dream of, yet he told me that at least one night a week, he dreamed that he was at his old job and facing a deadline or a sales quota only to wake up and realize he was retired. Even though I was in my late 20s, he would say, "Don't ever retire. It is worse than dying."

On one occasion when he had given me the "don't retire" lecture, I asked what motivated him to retire. I thought perhaps it was company policy or health reasons. He said that he worked for a large company in a Midwestern city. When he was 57 and his industry was facing major technological changes, the company he worked for sold to an international company. To continue to work for them required that he do a major career retooling. He would have to do more than take some refresher seminars; it would mean learning a new line of products, a new corporate culture, and a new set of government regulations. Recognizing his skills and contacts, the leaders from the new owner company invited and encouraged him to stay for ten more years. They told him they would pay for any retraining he needed.

Reynolds said that was overwhelmed with all the changes that he needed to make and had no clue where to start. He said, "If you don't know where to start, you must be at the end. I wish I had tried harder to find the place to begin."

A Person of Authentic Character

There are many midlifers who realize that they need and want to become people of authentic character. They have done a post mortem on the first half of life, and they see much evidence of diseased and infected character. The amount of deception, greed, lust, and jealousy they observe makes them wonder how they made it without being "outed" as a crook, fraud, pervert, or bad person. There are so many actions, attitudes, and habits they need to change, but they don't know where to start.

There are many voices calling out, "Start here." Each voice points to a different area. The physician says you start by taking care of your body through diet and exercise. Dr. Phil, Oprah, and the legion of self-help gurus say you begin with your attitude and thinking. The people at the local university promise you that if you enroll in their night course or weekend MBA program, you will be rich, sexy, happy, and a good person. The Internet pop-up screens and spam say you start with travel to exotic places, medicine for erotic pleasures, or yoga to escape chaotic pressure.

The television evangelist says you start by sending a check to Jesus; of course you do need to send it and make it payable to the name and address on the screen. The religious neighbors who pursue you with the fervor of a reformed drunk at a Budweiser convention promises you that authentic change starts with a religious experience very similar to theirs.

We do not lack advice on how to begin the process of becoming a good person. In fact, the confusing and contradicting nature of the possible solutions given is so overwhelming that we are tempted to hit the default key of status quo and stay in the same descending spiral.

The world is full of baby boomers who want to be better people and have a fundamental understanding of the destination of good character. Yet they have great difficulty in finding the right "on-ramp" for this journey that will take the last half of their lives. I know a gentleman who had serious neurological injuries in an automobile accident and had to learn how to walk again. He said during the long and tedious task of therapy he found that the fear was overwhelming. On some days, given the choice, he would have chosen to live the rest of his life using a wheelchair or a walker rather than face the fear of falling in his rehabilitation routine. He said each morning he found the first steps were the most difficult. When our entire life has been moving in the direction of success, and then after 40 years we deliberately turn toward goodness, we may find the first few steps are difficult.

Start with Subtraction/Addition

Most people assume they can become good through adding some actions and disciplines to their life. For the person who has some space available on their daily Outlook calendar, adding the time for relationships, community, and solitude can make significant progress in character development. However, most folks have no more space or energy in their lives, which is one of the reasons they are character depleted. Attempts to add to your life, even when the additive is good, character building, and positive, can be counter productive in that it causes emotional exhaustion, which leads to bad decisions, resulting in more character failure. An angry mother of two teenagers once told me that she could be a better mother if all of her time was not spent on cleaning up the problems her two valueless juvenile delinquents caused at school and in the community. She concluded, "Don't tell me to read one more book or attend another support group, and the only other doctor I will make an appointment with is named Kevorkian."

Most folks cannot add anything to their lives unless they also subtract something. As has been stated earlier, baby boomers live a faster pace than any previous generation. Because of the demands of aging parents and not-yet adult children, they are sandwiched and continually energy crunched.

The first thought is to begin deleting the things from the screen that we do not like to do and adding the things we enjoy doing. But this is a journey toward goodness, not necessarily toward comfort or ease. Instead, look at subtracting the actions and habits that are not only failing to produce goodness and character but that also contribute to our moral decline. It may even be something that once had value to us.

Jake was a successful entrepreneur who had taken a small mom-and-pop operation to levels far beyond expectation. Throughout the years when the pressure of work, the demands of his high-energy children, and concerns over an alcoholic brother became more than he could handle, he would go fishing. He had a small farm with a couple of fish-stocked ponds within 45 minutes of his office, and the routine of fishing refreshed him. But over the years, the fishing had become less therapeutic because he began fishing during the time he needed to develop strategies to cope with work

> "A driven person is usually caught in the uncontrolled pursuit of expansion."

and family. He was finding that he was coming home with more headaches than he went with. When Jake told his wife he was giving up fishing, she thought he was caving in to the pressure. Instead, he told her he was choosing to use the same time for some actions that could help him build character.

Janis was a fast-tracker in the financial industry who entered the workforce at age 32. She was a quick study who not only read technical books required by her chosen profession but also consumed self-help materials as if they were desserts for the mind. Materials on time management, relationships, marriage, and childrearing helped her to excel personally as well as professionally. Yet at age 45, she started finding that these self-help materials were becoming depressing because she couldn't do everything they suggested and the materials were often simplistic. The romantic breakfast-in-bed weekend did not add the expected spice to her middle-aged marriage, which carried scar tissue from neglect, normal aging, and accumulated missed expectations. The daily positive self-talk emails that she sent herself at ten, two, and four no longer provided the Dr. Pepper break for self-esteem that they once did. So she stopped reading self-help books and listening to the CDs in her car. While she was grateful for what they had added in years past, she needed a break from these. Instead, she used the time for journaling each day. At night she wrote down her thoughts, feelings, and reflections, and on the way to work did an audio journal that she shared with her husband.

The journey to goodness requires us to engage in meaningful individual relationships and authentic community; but in order to engage in these, we may need to escape from others that are counterproductive to the goal of goodness. In Gordon MacDonald's classic *Ordering Your Private World*, he states that, "A driven person is usually caught in the uncontrolled pursuit of expansion." While there have been driven people in all generations, baby boomers have often made it a calling and have given the wholesome-sounding name of "networking" to extending relationships and enlarging community. The thought of withdrawing from relationships and communities brings to mind the bittersweet concept of retirement. Midlifers are fond of saying, "Don't expect me to live in a condo in a Sun City and interpret card games and go the cafeteria for lunch." Instead, they expect to stay actively engaged until they are comatose. Yet more than one has told me that during the day they dread phone calls, email, and any conversation that makes them fully engage with people. A man pushing 50 told me the reason he likes participating in golf foursomes is because he can act as if he is engaged while living in his own little world. He continued, "Golf assumes you need silence to concentrate, when often the silence is feigned focus and is nothing more than a time to disengage."

Sometimes the first step to building meaningful relationships is to put some relationships behind you. Cade knew he wanted to really connect with his adult children. He realized that during their formative years he had neglected them while climbing his career ladder. After a few years of self-loathing and thinking it was too late, he realized his two adult children needed him more than ever. While feeling some responsibility for their shaky marriages and weak character, he saw an opportunity for redemption. But it would require him not to be so emotionally invested in being a caregiver at work. He realized that for many years he used his parenting skills with young employees instead of at home. So he made a commitment to stay engaged at work, but not to try to "parent" and mentor every entry-level executive. His open door policy at work needed to be revised to an "occasionally open door" that gave him more energy and engagement capacity in the evening and weekends when he was home with his family.

Others need to exit some communities before they join or engage in new communities. Being a member of a value-driven community in our society does not necessarily build and establish character, while being a participant in community does. We may have to leave some membership communities in order to become engaged in participating communities.

Several years ago a member of our church requested a meeting with me in my office. While I was well acquainted with her through her attendance at many functions in the church, she had never been to my office. During the small talk portion of our conversation, she was very nervous and I begin to think I was about to hear confession of sin, shame, and degradation. Finally she said, "Well, I am here to tell you I am leaving the church."

Her story was not a tale of sinful behavior but one that had roots in boredom. She said that she had gone through the motions at our church for several years, but she did not blame our church or our theology for apathy. Recently, she had started attending a small support group at a neighborhood church and then began attending their Sunday worship services. At the new church, she was being known for who she really was, and it was a freeing experience for her. For several months she attempted to attend both churches, but now felt she could grow more by disengaging formally from our congregation.

> *Finally she said, "Well, I am here to tell you I am leaving the church."*

While I didn't want our fellowship to lose her, she was most certainly doing the right thing. She was about 45 years old when she did this and now she is nearing 60. Her new church and community have empowered her to grow to the extent that she has changed careers, gone on mission trips, and finally removed some of the skid marks on her soul from a moral crash she had during her college years.

It is important to make sure that subtracting is not a way of running away or escaping what is painful or unpleasant. As is true in almost every other area of character development, accountability is needed when calculating the subtraction/addition factor. Trusted friends who are perceptive enough to know the difficult questions and confident enough to ask them are necessary to make this step meaningful and effective. It is important to never quit a longtime habit, even if it is a bad habit, without facing the question of "Why am I doing this?" The heart and mind can be deceptive, and they can be deceived even in the name of good character.

Adding Virtue

Let's suppose you have done some subtraction, and you are ready to add virtue to your life; where do you begin? Do you begin where you need the most help or in the area that feels like it might be easiest to change?

I find in my own life I need the feelings of progress to inspire more progress. Recently, an outstanding plastic surgeon who on occasion helps people with obesity problems by performing a mild weight reduction procedure was explaining how he worked with other physicians in determining when to do this procedure. He said while many assume that this shortcut to weight loss might discourage healthy eating and regular exercise habits, he has found that for many the exact reverse occurs. After losing ten pounds as a result of this procedure and experiencing progress, many individuals are now motivated to go to the next level regarding personal discipline. Success encourages success.

One of the easiest virtues to add with the greatest reward is gratitude. One aspect of the reward is the immediate affirmations you receive from others when you are grateful. This reward then motivates you not only to express gratitude but also to be authentically grateful. When people are receiving positive responses from others, it is easier to be grateful. Obviously if this is the only time you are grateful, your gratitude is more of a means than an end.

Recently I was invited to participate in a special Sunday night program at a local Catholic Church. After agreeing to speak and confirming in writing that I would be present, I realized that there was a meeting at our church that I really should attend. I knew there was no way to gracefully excuse myself from my participation at the Catholic Church because the event had been publicized in the community. I was frustrated with myself for agreeing to do it, realizing that my ministry associate had suggested that perhaps my schedule was already too full on that Sunday.

Not only was it a cold, damp, windy evening, but I made a wrong turn en route, which I allowed to darken my mood even more. Even though I thought I was late, I arrived 30 minutes before the actual program started and stood around making small talk, wishing I was at the meeting at my church. Just before the program was to begin, Father Pat Sullivan greeted me. It had been eight years since Father Pat and I had done a program together, and I was not even aware that he had been transferred to this parish. Father Pat is a character right out of a Bing Crosby movie. He has a contagious laugh, and he gives bear hugs rather than a handshakes. We briefly exchanged memories and pleasantries about the last time we were on a platform together, remembering that we had genuinely had a good time together. He told me how grateful he was that I could participate. He opened the program with prayer and then proceeded to tell his parish how fortunate they were to have the excellent special program commission who had done the planning for this event. He told them how personally grateful he was for all the guest speakers and what each of us meant to him as a brother in Christ. By the time I spoke, I was so glad I was there and I genuinely conveyed my gratitude in my speaking. It was a great evening that had been transformed by Father Pat's gratitude.

> *Gratitude is a great place to begin character renovation.*

Gratitude is a terrific place to begin a character renovation. When you are grateful, you will not only get immediate rewards but also begin to see character transformation in others. Gratitude will move people from the category of acquaintances to the circle of friends, as well as accelerate the bonding process.

I have found in my own life that gratitude is a self-fulfilling prophecy. When I am grateful, I genuinely want to develop character not only as a means of building relationships but also out of love for God. It is difficult, perhaps even impossible, for people to be ungrateful and love God. If you don't love God, the desire for character development will only be a pragmatic issue; your perceived better character helps you get what you selfishly want. It isn't really goodness you seek, only the appearance of goodness.

In addition to knowing where to begin the journey toward becoming a good person, the journey must be perceived as a lifelong process. While the basic core values of character can and should be firmly implanted in our souls, our understanding of how to apply them will be continually changing because we are changing.

Unfortunately, we often discuss change as if it were only a preferable behavioral pattern in life. Change is not an option and is inevitable. What is optional is the nature and direction of the change. Everyone is changing and the pressing issue is not if or when, but do we choose to change in ways that are good or ways that are bad.

Lifelong Learning

A commitment to become a better person is also a commitment to lifelong learning. Midlife is not when we need to start changing but a great opportunity to be deliberately aware of the power of intentional change. A very vibrant 78-year-old member of my church moved to a retirement center several years ago. I asked how she liked it there, and she said, "I like it. I liked living in my own home. I liked living with my husband when he was alive. I have liked every stage of my adult life since I was 32 years of age."

I asked what happened at age 32. On New Year's Day of that year, her husband was transferred by the government for a three year term of duty, or as she preferred to think of it, a "sentence," to a sparsely populated state. It was winter, and the only color she saw during January was on a billboard advertising Winston cigarettes. She told her husband that she thought the state's official color was drab and its official motto should be "Where boredom begins." She was absolutely miserable and passed on her emotions to her husband and their two small children.

Her sometimes irreverent and spunky mother, who had raised her kids during the Depression, was tired of receiving phone calls and letters bemoaning where her daughter's lot in life had taken her. The mother sent her daughter the following two sentence letter: "You have the choice to either bloom where you are planted or die. I hope you make the right choice; if not, let me know so I can return your birthday presents within the 30 days allowed by J.C. Penney's." Now, 46 years later, the mature woman in the retirement center said, "I realized my mother was right and that my misery was self-imposed and revealed more about me than the forsaken state in which we were living."

As much as baby boomers hate to admit it and work to deny it, old age and the senior adult years are coming. If you think our parents and our older siblings despised the label of "senior adult," just wait until some attempt is made to give that nametag to our generation. We will squeal like our mother's hearing device when that dreaded moniker is attached to us. Retirement centers and convalescent care facilities are already being marketed as adult enrichment centers, and at least one such center now provides a surgical procedure center on their campus for certain types of minor cosmetic surgery. But we are aging!

Get in the Habit

If we are not in the habit of character development in midlife, we probably will not be in the last quarter of life. It is possible to begin the intentional character development before we begin the last lap on the track of life, but is it is unlikely.

One of the long-time myths of character building is that if you are doing it right, it is exciting. Add to this the more recent myth taught by some mid-twentieth century educators and fostered by book publishers that learning is always fun. As a result, we saw many schools attempt to find ways to "fun up" learning. In the process, however, they sometimes "dumbed down" education. Neither is character building or learning always a fun process. For the first few stages of the process, you may find it requires more than it gives.

An educator who founded a private high school based on the classical learning philosophies said the most difficult thing is to get people to understand that education is work. Make no mistake, some learning can be fun, but much of it involves repetition. It has been mistakenly said that practice makes perfect. A more accurate statement is that practice makes permanent. Many of the attempts to make character development fun are nothing more than providing a sweet-tasting placebo with the false promise that it will do the work of chemotherapy on the cancer of your soul.

The commitment to become a good person of wholesome character is not a cure for a midlife crisis any more than a marriage vow is a cure for lust. While aging is not for the faint of heart, becoming a woman of valor or a man of character is not for the weak or for those who lack stamina. It is for the person who is willing to wake up every morning with a passion to become more of what God had in mind when one day He said, "Let us make man in our image, in our likeness, and let them rule over the fish of the sea and the birds of the air, over the livestock, over all the earth, and over all the creatures that move along the ground. So God created man in his own image, in the image of God he created him; male and female he created them" (Genesis 1:26–27).

The commitment to character building is even more demanding than the vow to become a lifelong learner because it requires the dedication to change. Learning can simply be the acquiring of knowledge; goodness requires lifelong change in attitude and action. One of the dirty little secrets about change is that meaningful change requires loss. If change were entirely about gain, we would pursue it the way the way government craves taxes. People do not resist change, but they resist loss. We resist change because we do not like to give up the patterns and habits that make our life comfortable and predictable. It is difficult to change even when we fully understand the logic and rationale that fuel the change.

The city in which I live, Birmingham, Alabama, is often noted for racial prejudice because of well-publicized events that happened nearly 50 years ago. While we still have room for progress in racial reconciliation, significant progress has been achieved in race relations. The church is

> *The commitment to become a good person of wholesome character is not a cure for a midlife crisis any more than a marriage vow is a cure for lust.*

often accused of being the slowest institution to reflect racial change, or as more than one social critic has said, "11:00 A.M. on Sunday is the most segregated hour of the week." I'm not sure that generalization is totally accurate, but it's close enough to truth to be accepted as conventional wisdom. Yet in our city, there are encouraging signs that fly in the face of the public perception. We have predominantly African American churches in our city with some white staff members, and 99% white congregations with some African American staff members. The church I serve as pastor, while definitely a white majority congregation, has without controversy or even comment had African Americans in key leadership positions, including ministerial staff and chair of deacons. We are changing.

On a cold winter Tuesday evening as I was on my way home, I knew I needed to make a hospital visit to check on an elderly gentleman. It had been a long, full day, and I really wanted to go home. On Tuesday mornings I meet with a small prayer group at 6:40 A.M., have staff meetings, and then have planning meetings with worship leaders. This particular year, I was also teaching a late Tuesday afternoon class on leadership at the seminary in our city. My topic in class for that day had been "Leading Change." During the class presentation, I knew that I needed to be practicing what I was teaching. We needed to add a third worship service on Sunday morning, which in turn would cause a change in Sunday school times.

Five years earlier, we changed the Sunday morning schedule by adding an additional early morning Sunday school, and although the change was effective, it was not without pain. This additional morning worship not only changed the church's schedule but would also change my routine and to some extent my position. These changes would directly impact staff assignments and the skill sets and passions of future staff members.

Leaving class that day, I had thought to myself, "Can I lead this change process?" I knew I needed to for the good of the church, and I knew that now was the time. But I was really not as concerned with the organizational change as I was with the change that I knew I needed to make. While few in the church realized it, I knew this new service would be a catalyst requiring to me to make a major change in the way I do ministry.

The church I was serving and the world around us had changed significantly in the last few years. I knew it would be easy to postpone the change and few would object. Yet, I was also aware that failure to lead through these changes was a character issue. It bothered me that I knew what the right thing was but that I was resisting. I am a pastor and I even get paid to be good, yet the good was something I was dreading.

With these thoughts filling the crevices of my mind, I had just about convinced myself I did not need to make this hospital visit. I decided to make a perfunctory pastoral call. I would put on my best smile, act like I was listening, and then when there was a pause in the conversation, say, "Let me lead us in a word of prayer." I have often used the line that in the original Greek, "prayer" means the last thing a preacher does before exiting a room.

But the visit took a very sharp change in direction as soon as I entered the room. The gentleman said he hoped someone from the church would stop by because he needed to visit about an issue in his life. He began by telling of being a young man in the south and working in one of the first integrated companies and of the pride he felt in having participated in a small way in the racial progress. His company was one of the first to utilize African Americans in leadership positions, even though people warned his company president that if they promoted minorities, there would be trouble.

There were no protests. It was a non-event. He said that while there were television camera crews filming the attempts to integrate the downtown lunch counters, their company's lunchroom was quietly but fully integrated. But he said he had one major regret for something he had done. He spoke softly, with emotion dripping off his whispered words as if he were about to confess an atrocity. Knowing that there are many dark secrets from this era of life in our city, I did not know what to expect. He said, "When I worked for the company, I followed an unwritten rule that whites and blacks never shook hands. We greeted each other each day and used first names, but we did not shake hands. Why did I comply with such an evil prejudice and practice and not have the courage to do right? I would not have been fired and may have experienced some minor ridicule, but regardless of the response, it would have been the right thing to do. Although I never discussed it with anyone, I knew what I was doing was wrong." He paused and asked, "Why did I so easily give into the fears and choose comfort over my convictions? I am not a racist; why did I do that?"

> *"When I worked for the company, I followed an unwritten rule that whites and blacks never shook hands."*

The elderly patient told me that he had made it a point since retirement to shake hands with every minority he met. He said, "I have extended my hand to everyone that comes in this hospital room, and some probably think I'm just a lonely old man who needs a touch, but this is about being a changed man, not a lonely man." After he finished speaking, we just sat in silence for a few minutes while he grieved for the past, and then I led in a prayer acknowledging God's forgiveness and asking God to help us both be changed men.

If this 89-year-old man could make changes in character, so could I. I knew I too would have to face my fears and make the changes. Whatever stage of life we are in, fear is the greatest enemy of change. Perhaps that is why the command "Fear not" is stated 365 times in the Bible. One for every day of the year!

Recently a lady asked me if I thought Jesus had a mid-life crisis, and how did I suppose He would handle the aging process. I did not have an answer for her and made some type of meaningless statement that allowed us go to another subject.

Since then, I have been thinking about her two questions and realize that they are related. Midlife crises are often the result of realizing that there is an end to the tunnel and then trying to decide whether we need slow down to avoid crashing into the end or to spend up and break through the end. Jesus was fully aware that the cross was the wall at the end of the tunnel, but rather than slowing down, Jesus chose to hit the wall the same way He lived, and that was with the redemption of humanity as His purpose.

While our character does not redeem humanity, our lives are to continually announce there is a Redeemer who has broken through the end of tunnel for all people. Midlife is a time to accelerate. It is now that we know, even though it appears to be dark at end the tunnel, it is only the darkness that precedes the sunrise of Easter Sunday morning. Because of the reality of the resurrection, we can go full speed to the end, seeking good for goodness' sake.

SIMILAR BOOKS YOU MAY ENJOY

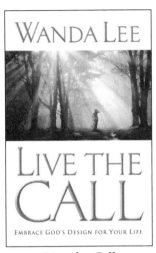

Live the Call
Embrace God's Design for Your Life
By Wanda Lee
ISBN 1-56309-994-2

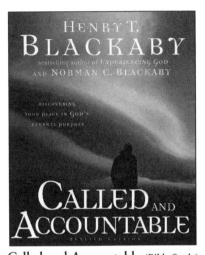

Called and Accountable (Bible Study)
*Discovering Your Place
in God's Eternal Purpose*
By Henry T. Blackaby
and Norman C. Blackaby
ISBN 1-56309-946-2

I Have Called You Friends
*New Testament Images That Challenge Us
to Live as Christ Followers*
By Fisher Humphreys
ISBN 1-56309-945-4

new
hope
PUBLISHERS

Available in bookstores everywhere

For information about these books
or any New Hope products, visit
www.newhopepublishers.com.

New Hope® Publishers is a division of WMU®,
an international organization that challenges Christian
believers to understand and be radically involved in
God's mission. For more information about WMU,
go to www.wmu.com. More information
about New Hope books may be found at
www.newhopepublishers.com. New Hope books
may be purchased at your local bookstore.